KT-466-010

Space Place Life

The Academy of Urbanism

Edited by Brian Evans and Frank McDonald

LEARNING FROM PLACE 1

Routledge
Taylor & Francis Group

LONDON AND NEW YORK

THE ACADEMY OF URBANISM

First edition published 2007
by RIBA Publishing

This edition published 2011
by Routledge
2 Park Square, Milton Park, Abingdon, Oxon OX14 4RN

Simultaneously published in the USA and Canada
by Routledge 711 Third Avenue, New York, NY 10017

Routledge is an imprint of the Taylor & Francis Group, an informa business

© 2011 Academy of Urbanism

The right of The Academy of Urbanism to be identified as author of this work has
been asserted by him/her in accordance with sections 77 and 78 of the Copyright,
Designs and Patents Act 1988.

All rights reserved. No part of this book may be reprinted or reproduced or utilised in
any form or by any electronic, mechanical, or other means, now known or hereafter
invented, including photocopying and recording, or in any information storage or
retrieval system, without permission in writing from the publishers.

British Library Cataloguing in Publication Data
A catalogue record for this book is available from the British Library

Library of Congress Cataloging-in-Publication Data
Space, Place, Life: Learning from Place 1 / Academy of Urbanism;
Edited by Brian Evans, Frank McDonald.

p. cm.
1. Urbanization. 2. Cities and towns. 3. City planning 4. Sociology, Urban.
I. Evans, B. M. (Brian M.) II. McDonald, Frank, 1950 Jan. 24-
III. Academy of Urbanism (Organization)
HT166.S6352 2011
307.76--dc22
2010050634

ISBN13: 978-0-415-61399-6 (hbk)
ISBN13: 978-0-415-61400-9 (pbk)

Typeset in Helvetica Neue LT Std by
URBED
Printed and bound in Great Britain by Ashford Colour Press Ltd

University of Strathclyde
Dept of Architecture
Library

Space Place Life

Space Place Life is the first in a series of books drawing on the expertise of The Academy of Urbanism. This book examines the concepts that are core to the academy: the way that urban space is designed, the quality place created by the buildings that enclose this space and the life that animates it. All great towns and cities across the world depend on these three fundamental aspects of urban life.

The Academy of Urbanism brings together architects, urban designers, planners, surveyors, economists, academics and developers to better understand what makes successful urban places. This first book in what is to become a series includes contributions from some of the leading thinkers in the field including the television documentary maker Jonathan Meades and the Irish architectural journalist Frank McDonald.

This is combined with essays by leading urban practitioners inspired by the places shortlisted for the Academy's first ever awards. The surveyor Chris Balch writes about three capital cities: Dublin, Edinburgh and London. The urban designer David Rudlin is fascinated by the sense of belonging and community found in the shortlisted towns while the public realm designer Brian Evans takes a walk through three great neighbourhoods. The highway engineer David Taylor becomes an urbanist to explore the life of three great streets while the academic Sarah Chaplin responds to three very different urban places.

The book is a fascinating take on urban places and the forces that animate them, written by some of the most experienced urban practitioners in the UK and illustrated beautifully with drawings by David (Harry) Harrison and poems by Ian McMillan.

D307.76 EVA

Contents

Cockburn Street Edinburgh

John Thompson

Foreword

For generation after generation, in many different cultures and in many different climates, people came together and created places that uniquely reflected their collective needs.

And then we lost the art of place-making.

Without it, the life of the individual is blighted, the life of the community is stillborn and the future of the planet is jeopardised.

With it, people can find expression for their own creativity, communities can develop their own vision and leadership and the planet can be secured for the enjoyment of future generations.

In this first book in the Learning from Place series we present 15 Great Places at the level of the City, Town, Neighbourhood, Street and Place.

Each place is the result of an appropriate and legible ordering of space for the purpose of personal and public exchange – social, cultural, spiritual and economic – in a way that enhances the life of both the individual and the community.

Some are old; some are new; some have looked after themselves through changing times; some have benefited from timely and life-saving interventions; all are united by their ability to learn.

Through the relationships that are being established with each of these places, the Academy is seeking to create a body of evidence-based enquiry that can inform our quest to identify and deliver best practice in Urbanism.

Great places have the power to fire the imagination of their citizens. No one can create them on their own. If, collectively, we are to create them once again, we must first share a common view.

This is the mission of the Academy.

John Thompson,
Chairman, The Academy of Urbanism
2007

Acknowledgements

From the outset, it has been a mission for The Academy of Urbanism to record and document what might be learnt about Cities, Towns, Neighbourhoods, Streets and Places by studying the shortlisted entries for the Urbanism Awards each year. This exercise is almost more important than the Awards themselves. By definition, one city is different from the next, one neighbourhood the antithesis of another and so on. Learning from Place 1 is our first attempt to document this important pedagogic mission for the Academy: Where we begin to assemble the evidence in such a way that, following a number of years of the Awards, we might be able to set out an explicit view of what constitutes a great city, town, neighbourhood, street and place in these islands.

This task would have been impossible without the commitment, time, insight and understanding of those who manage and maintain the shortlisted places as well as those who visited, studied and documented the shortlist of three in each category.

In the three cities, Trevor Davies, Riccardo Marini, Malcolm Fraser, Gillian Tee and Sandra Elgin provided understanding, knowledge and insight into Edinburgh; as did Dick Gleeson, Margaret Coyle, Margaret Gormley, James Pike and Tony Reddy in Dublin; and Patricia Brown, Jennifer O'Brien, Eddie Nelms, Tim Waterman and Chris Brett in London.

With the towns, Peter Studdert, Rachael Morris, Cathy Robertson, David Chiddick, Derek Cottrell, Gary Cooke, Robin Peak, Muriel Robertson, Rob Bradley, Keith Laidler, Amanda Batham, Keren Hickerton, Kathy Holland, Debbie Butcher and Ken Round gave of their time and knowledge for Lincoln; as did Tim King, Graeme Kidd, Ann Holland, Helen Duce, Paul Russell, Colin Richardson, Melanie Revolta and Bob Young for Ludlow; and Richard Shaw, Bill Fry, David Rutherford, Malcolm Veal, C.J. Trier, Ian Bailey, Tamsin Daniel, David Scott, David Hampshire and Peter Butts for St. Ives.

Gordon Mathieson, Gerry Grams, Liz Davidson, Ewan Curtis, Steve Insch, Alan Sproull, Polly Mayes, Ross Hunter, Peter McGowan, Ronnie Maclellan and David Porter coordinated and organised the visit and study of the Merchant City; as did Sasha Lubetkin, Julia Killingback, Richard Parnaby, Sarah Williams and George Ferguson in Clifton; and Peter Murray, Chris Brett, Alan Baxter and David Pritchard in Clerkenwell.

Jonathan Nichols, Marcus Wilshere, Patricia Holmes and Ann Short organised the Academy's study of Brick Lane; as did Andrew Ashenden, Brenda Levey, Martin Whittles, Martin Low, Rosemarie MacQueen, Trevor Osborne and Susan Parhan for Marylebone High Street; and the Edinburgh City people obliged with the Royal Mile.

Clifton, Bristol

Finally, Clive Dutton, Louise Murphy, Philip Singleton, Gary Taylor, Joe Holyoak, Noha Nasser and Peter Lee provided the material and organised the visit for Brindleyplace; George Nicholson, Simone Crofton, Juliet Barclay, Ken Grieg and John East did so for Borough Market; and the Dublin City people extended their knowledge and time to include St. Stephen's Green.

The Academy would also like to thank Ian McMillan for his poems; David 'Harry' Harrison for his sketches; Rebecca Taylor, Joe Wood, Alice Leeves and the team at John Thompson & Partners for preparing the figure-ground drawings and sourcing aerial photographs; and everyone at RIBA Publishing who worked on the original edition – Steven Cross, Anna Walters, Karen Willcox for Aleatoria and Susan George.

We would like to thank Linda Gledstone and Angela Whitehouse (and early on Carrie Smith) for their tireless and good-natured work in support of the work of the Academy.

Finally, Frank and Brian would like to thank all the other authors for their long evenings of hard work spent putting the chapters together.

Contributors

Professor Chris Balch is from West Somerset. He studied geography at Sidney Sussex, Cambridge and urban design and regional planning at Edinburgh University, later qualifying as a Chartered Town Planner and Surveyor. He has more than 30 years experience working in both local government and private consultancy, with a particular interest in urban regeneration and large-scale development projects. He advised government on the Leeds Development Corporation in the late 1980's and subsequent proposals for Housing Action Trust in Leeds, Hull and Tower Hamlets as well as on the funding of major Millennium projects including the Lowry Arts complex at Salford Quays, the Millennium Stadium in Cardiff, the Odyssey Project in Belfast and the Forum in Norwich. Internationally he has worked in Bahrain, Malaysia, Pakistan and the Czech Republic. He was Managing Director of DTZ in the UK and Chair of Basildon Renaissance Partnership, one of the local delivery agencies in the Thames Gateway. He is now Professor of Planning at the University of Plymouth. He is a founding Academician at The Academy of Urbanism.

Sarah Chaplin is a Partner at Evolver LLP, a strategic design consultancy, and is currently facilitating the conceptual development of the Battersea Power Station site with JTP Cities. She was a founding member of both The Academy of Urbanism and the Architectural Humanities Research Association, and served as a national research assessor for Architecture and Built Environment for RAE 2008. She is a CABE enabler and an external examiner at the Bartlett and the University of Edinburgh. She was formerly deputy director of the Urban Renaissance Institute and prior to that was head of the School of Architecture and Landscape at Kingston University for six years. She has published, lectured and broadcast widely on urbanism, visual culture, Japanese cultural history and contemporary architecture. She is the author of Japanese Love Hotels (Routledge, 2007) and co-editor of Curating Architecture and the City (Routledge, 2009).

Brian Evans is from St. Andrews and was educated at Edinburgh and Strathclyde universities. Since 1989, he has been a partner of Gillespies, leading landscape design and regeneration projects in the UK, Scandinavia, Russia, the Middle East and China. From 2004 until 2010, he was Deputy Chair of Architecture+Design Scotland and before that a CABE enabler. He was previously a member of the City of Sheffield's Urban Design Review Panel and is now co-chair of the City's Sustainable Development & Design Panel. He is co-author of Tomorrow's Architectural Heritage (Mainstream, 1991) and urban design adviser for Making Cities Work (Wiley, 2003). He has taught widely at architecture schools in Britain and continental Europe. From 1998 until 2004, he was Artistic Professor of Urban Design at Chalmers University School of Architecture in Gothenburg. In 2008 he was made an honorary professor at the Mackintosh School of Architecture, Glasgow School of Art and in 2010 was invited to become Head of Urbanism there. He is a co-founder and a director of the Academy of Urbanism.

David (Harry) Harrison is a Partner at John Thompson & Partners and an architect with a wide experience of urban design and community planning in both the private and public sectors, throughout the UK and Europe. His projects include award-winning schemes at Barnes Waterside and Putney Wharf in London and at Charter Quay in Kingston-upon-Thames. He is from Norwich and is The Academy of Urbanism's Artist-in-Residence. His paintings and drawings have been displayed at the Royal Academy's Summer Exhibition.

Frank McDonald is from Dublin and lives in Temple Bar, the city's 'cultural quarter'. Educated at St. Vincent's CBS Glasnevin and University College Dublin, he is Environment Editor of The Irish Times, having been the newspaper's Environment Correspondent since 1986. He has won several awards, including one for Outstanding Work in Irish Journalism for a series of articles in 1979 entitled 'Dublin - What Went Wrong?'. He is the author of The Destruction of Dublin (Gill and Macmillan, 1985) and Saving the City (Tomar, 1989), two books that helped to change Irish public policy on urban renewal. More recently, he co-authored Ireland's Earthen Houses (A. A. Farmer, 1997) and edited The Ecological Footprint of Cities (International Institute for the Urban Environment, 1997). His third book on Dublin, The Construction of Dublin (Gandon, 2000), became a non-fiction bestseller. He is also joint author with James Nix of Chaos at the Crossroads (Gandon, 2005), a book documenting the environmental destruction of Ireland. In October 2006, he was awarded an honorary DPhil by Dublin Institute of Technology.

Ian McMillan is Poet-in-Residence for The Academy of Urbanism, English National Opera, and Barnsley FC. He is UK Trade & Investment's Poet, Yorkshire TV's Investigative Poet and Humberside Police's Beat Poet. He is a regular on Pick of the Week, The Arts Show, The Today Programme, You & Yours and Have I Got News For You. Ian is Visiting Professor at Bolton University and is an honorary doctor of Sheffield Hallam University, Staffordshire University and most recently, University Centre Barnsley - Huddersfield University. Ian has helped to judge the John Betjeman Young People's Poetry Competition and has toured with his acclaimed verse autobiography Talking Myself Home (John Murray Publishers, 2008) and The Ian McMillan Orchestra, featured on The South Bank Show. He also presents A Cartoon History of Here with several times Cartoonist of The Year Tony Husband, and Flipchart & Squeezebox projects with Orchestra ring-leader, Luke Carver Goss. Ian has been a poet, broadcaster, commentator and programme maker for over 25 years. He has explored language & communication with students, teachers, policy makers, local authority officers, politicians and business communities.

Jonathan Meades was born and brought up in Salisbury. He spent four years at school in Taunton, where he learnt about scrumpy and shirking. He subsequently went to RADA. He lived until 2006 in central London, when he moved to beyond the back of beyond near Bordeaux, in order to devote himself to conversations about combine harvesters. He is the author of several books including three works of fiction - Filthy English (Cape, 1984), Pompey and The Fowler Family Business (Fourth Estate, 2002) - and two anthologies of journalism Peter Knows What Dick Likes (Paladin Grafton, 1989) and Incest and Morris Dancing (Cassells Illustrated, 2002). He is currently working on a book entitled An Encyclopaedia of Myself. He has written and performed in some fifty television shows on predominantly topographical subjects such as self-built shacks, the utopian avoidance of right angles, the lure of vertigo, the deleterious effects of garden cities, the buildings occasioned by beer, Birmingham's appeal, megastructures, Worcestershire and the everyday surrealism of Belgium; some of these are available on The Jonathan Meades Collection DVD. 'Magnetic North' (2008) - a journey from Flanders to Helsinki - was described by Robert Hanks in The Independent as having 'a sweep, an intellectual confidence and a sense of mischief you won't find anywhere else on TV. Meades is an artist of television.' The 2009 series Off Kilter was described by Simon Heffer in the Daily Telegraph as 'a masterpiece'. He has been described by Will Buckley in The Observer as 'by furlongs the most erudite broadcaster of the age' and by Time Out as 'a heavily sedated Sir Geoffrey Howe.'

Professor Kevin Murray is a chartered town planner and urbanist, and a Past President of the Royal Town Planning Institute. Educated at Aberdeen University and Oxford Brookes University, Kevin is a co-founder, director and now Chair of The Academy of Urbanism. Beginning his career at the London Borough of Bromley, he joined Tibbalds Partnership in 1985 and EDAW ten years later, before starting his own practice in 2002. He has been involved in development, regeneration and conservation projects all across the UK, many involving innovative leadership in placemaking, such as the award-winning 'place momentum' engagement process. He was co author of the groundbreaking New Vision for Planning (RTPI, 2001) and also helped found the Urban Design Alliance (UDAL). He served on the Egan Task Group on Skills for Sustainable Communities and as a board member of the Academy for Sustainable Communities (ASC). An occasional media contributor on urbanism, Kevin was the focus of BBC Radio 4's Cities in 2010 and an adviser on Channel 4's Big Art programme. He is Honorary Professor of Planning at Glasgow University.

David Rudlin manages URBED (Urbanism Environment and Design). He is a planner by training and started his career with the city council in his home town of Manchester, working on the redevelopment of the Hulme estate. He was a founder member of the Homes for Change Housing Cooperative which built one of the flagship buildings in Hulme and co-wrote the Hulme Guide to Development. He joined URBED in 1990 to manage the award-winning Little Germany project in Bradford. Since then he has managed a range of projects including Temple Quay 2 in Bristol, The New England Quarter in Brighton and the UK's fourth Millennium Village in Telford. He is

the author of reports including 21st Century Homes for the Joseph Rowntree Foundation, Tomorrow a peaceful path to urban reform for Friends of the Earth and But would you live there? for the Urban Task Force. This writing is summarised in Sustainable Urban Neighbourhood published by the Architectural Press and described by Richard Rogers as 'the best analysis (he) had read of the crisis facing the contemporary city'. David has been a member of the CABE Design Review Committee and a trustee of CUBE (the Centre for the Understanding of the Built Environment) in Manchester. He has been judge for the CNU awards in the US and the Europan Awards. He is an Academician of The Academy of Urbanism and is currently chair of the Sheffield Design Panel and BEAM in Wakefield.

David Taylor is a Senior Director at Alan Baxter and Associates. He leads the practice's work on masterplanning, urban design, transport and the public realm. He has a profound belief in the value that good design can bring to urbanism. His extensive experience includes major urban studies, city-scale master planning and re-generation projects, urban extensions, infill and new self-contained settlements. David is a key contributor to major public consultation events, and has led the authorship of a number of publications on urban design. He has a wealth of experience on a wide range of projects. His work for DCLG and CABE informed development policy in the Thames Gateway region and he has also been involved in the characterisation of settlement patterns in the Cambridge and Midlands areas. At Ashford, David led the movement aspects of the Local Development Framework, aimed at handling the growth of the region from a population of 60,000 to 120,000 over the course of 25 years. This involved strategic work leading to the design of major infrastructure projects and the reworking of the Ashford ring road as an urban street.

John Thompson is the Founder-Chairman of The Academy of Urbanism, and Chairman of John Thompson and Partners, one of Europe's leading firms of architects and urbanists. In the 1980s he pioneered the use of Community Planning in the United Kingdom as a tool for engaging local people in the design of their neighbourhoods and has subsequently led a series of seminal projects that have simultaneously delivered physical, social and economic change. He was formerly chairman of the RIBA's Urbanism and Planning Group and a founding member of The Urban Villages Forum, and is currently a member of Yorkshire Forward's Urban and Rural Renaissance Panels. John has undertaken masterplanning and urban design projects in towns and cities throughout the UK and Europe. He is currently designing a series of new settlements in England, Scotland, Iceland, Moscow City Region and China.

Kevin Murray

Whither an Academy of Urbanism?

Who needs another body promoting urbanism? And why should it be an Academy? Are professional bodies not already addressing this? Doesn't the government have a range of policy and training initiatives on this now? What is different about our initiative? What are we doing, why and to what end?

These are the questions we discussed, debated and tested each other with during 2005, as The Academy of Urbanism took shape to fill its own unique role. Convening at the RIBA in London, sometimes during bomb alerts, conversing over dinner with fellow travellers, and reflecting by phone and email, we shaped not only an organisational entity but – more importantly – a philosophical outlook and a set of principles.

Our diverse group of individuals, convened by George Ferguson and John Thompson, was drawn not only from architecture and urban design, but from the worlds of academia and research, planning and economic development, property investment and housebuilding. This range and reach grew as we captured the imagination of many potential supporters and, although initially cautious, many public sector policymakers saw a benefit if we could reach out to developers and housebuilders – helping them build and regenerate place-communities, not just schemes, projects and buildings.

Positive and enduring place-making is important to all of us, with many being actively involved in the design, management and renewal of towns, neighbourhoods, streets and spaces. Some are involved in framing policy, others in research and critique, including judging for awards. Several were active in earlier efforts at positive place-making, such as the Urban Villages Forum and the Urban Design Alliance. Drawing on these, and on the enlightening

Ancient and modern Istanbul.

experiences some of us had in Yorkshire Forward's Renaissance Panel, together with visits to old and new exemplars of urbanism in Europe and America, we came to the same conclusion that Francis Tibbalds alighted on in *Making People-friendly Towns*[1] – namely that *places matter most*.

This is particularly so in the globalised post-industrial world, where people can choose to live, work and visit almost anywhere. No longer geographically rooted by the locations of old industries, mineral reserves, or agricultural or fishery produce, our towns and cities have to find new roles to survive and prosper. Identity, image and 'brand' marketing are now commonly part of civic armoury as cities compete in the 'knowledge age' league tables. The influencing media have moved well beyond the texts of Baedeker, Pevsner and the Lonely Planet guides, which provided thoughtful interpretations, to the more immediate digital worlds of film, television, music, video and now podcasts.

Although movies such as *Manhattan, Sleepless in Seattle* and *Amelie* integrated evocative place imagery into their narrative, many cities have been reduced to negative, one-dimensional caricatures about crime, drugs, race or unemployment. Such media reductionism has been refracted through many filters to produce major identity challenges for the likes of Glasgow, Liverpool, Marseilles, Berlin,

Chicago and Istanbul, potentially affecting tourism and inward investment. Many cities now seek to turn these reductionist tables with iconic building imagery and strapline graphics in adverts and online, stripping down their character of place to fit the simplistic marketing needs of the digital age.

While changes in technology and the potential impact on city identity are recognised, true urbanism, as espoused by our Academy, needs to look much deeper, to understand and then influence change positively. Indeed, if we

Downtown Chicago

are to stand any chance of improving the urban habitat that now accommodates over 50% of the world's population, and thereby make an impact on bigger global issues such as quality of life, social justice and climate change, we need to move on from the rationalised modernist views that deconstructed so many towns and cities in the 20th century. We cannot just look at the world through the simplified quasi-professional prisms of transportation systems, land use zoning or economic development through sequences of property deals. Such outmoded, segmentalised systems-thinking sadly influences urban policy and practice even today. England's Housing Market Renewal programme, for instance, is essentially a closed system approach, mitigating against holistic solutions in urban regeneration.

We need to unpack and reconstitute the synoptic art of city-making that was substantially lost during the so-called *machine age* of the 20th century. Although the 'clean break' of early modern movements can be appreciated in the context of forward-looking technological progress after the traumas of the First World War, it soon wreaked havoc on cities, even small towns, and also on our collective sense of what urban settlements could or should be. The fanciful

Western Harbour, Malmö.

creativity of Fritz Lang's *Metropolis* sadly represented the oppressive nightmare that was life for so many people living in over-industrialised cities. Too many uncritically adopted technological functionalism as the way forward.

In reflecting on this earlier traumatic era of competing ideologies, a key distinction may be drawn between modernism in art, music and literature and how it came to be applied in architecture and urban planning. The over-rationalisation around a few narrow principles, including the alleged pursuit of neo-Platonic universal truth, and the reduction of design challenges down to one or two core functionalist ideas, constituted a hubris that created profound impacts as the philosophies of influential urban modernists were played out in the public realm across the world. Though some of the great modernist architects – Le Corbusier, Alvar Aalto, Frank Lloyd Wright and Mies van der Rohe – could brilliantly combine interiors and furniture design into their unified idea of architecture, they singularly failed in their work at the city place-making scale. Having been used to controlling all variables in their clear but limited functionalist programme at the scale of a building, the innate flaws of modernism's simplicity were exposed at a grander scale. Le Corbusier's *Ville Radieuse* approach, with its denial of the role of the street, which he wanted to kill off, and the vertical perversion of the traditional neighbourhood, is perhaps the best-known exemplar of this terrible trend. Tragically, his ideas were pursued by civic architects, planners and highway engineers across the globe for much of the later 20th century. Perhaps only now do we regard the criticisms offered by Lewis Mumford and Jane Jacobs as representing a more legitimate and wiser strand of thinking.

Western Harbour, Malmö.

When applied in urban place-making, modernism was simply not open or adaptable enough to encompass alternative conceptions of reality. There was not the room for the complex and contradictory richness of real places – the messy and unwelcome past or any unimagined transformative future. Trapped in the straightjacket of its own zeitgeist, modernist urban planning did not allow for changed principles, preferences and ideologies that are so inevitable in the urban realm.

In other spheres, modernism seemed to involve a break with tradition that was ultimately able to co-exist alongside antecedents. Joyce does not wipe out Trollope or Dickens by re-thinking the novel; nor do Schoenberg or Miles Davis supplant Mozart. Picasso and Braque can be viewed in a gallery alongside Old Masters. This compatibility was not the case with so much modern civic architecture and planning, especially when augmented by highway infrastructure that focused on the primacy of vehicle movement above all else. Historic city quarters were blitzed to accommodate new roads, bridges, ports and economic infrastructure – their very contemporary design purposefully paying no regard to historical context.

Real enduring towns and cities are complex and mutli-layered, necessarily absorbing changes across generations, regimes and even religious upheaval. They are neither mono-use nor mono-cultural. Unlike most modernist architecture, they are actually enhanced by the redundancy of original purpose. It is the adaptive reprogramming, reinterpretation and recycling that is part of the appeal of, for instance, Berlin, Istanbul, Milan, New York and Seville. They are not made up of a single idea, and their ability to change roles demonstrates the robustness of good urbanism.

It is the current failure to address adequately the many facets of successful urbanism that drives our Academy to research, understand and learn from the places that work for a wide range of people. If, as Sir Patrick Geddes asserted, 'a city is more than a place in space … it is a drama in time,' we need to appreciate that urbanism is more than design and buildings, and create a long-term template to nurture and interact with the drama.

In this early part of the 21st century, there are some grounds for being optimistic about better urbanism. Cities like Copenhagen and Barcelona have been recognised for their achievements in turning around their urban liveability, while many others follow to attract skills, talent, investment and tourism. There is always the pressure to retreat into such strategems as commissioning signature 'starchitects', megaschemes or simplistic identity-branding campaigns and we must also be wary of shallow urbanism aimed at short-term votes rather than long-term liveability.

As a reflective body, our Academy therefore seeks to *learn from place,* as our starting point, rather than from policies, plans, city administrators or professionals, though they may all have contributed somewhere along the line. We recognise successful places through our awards at different scales. Our first cohort of winners provides the focus of this book.

By adopting this place-based approach, we are also able to appreciate the role of historic contributions in urban design, infrastructure planning or land management, all of which may have been important ingredients of current success – for instance, by setting down a framework for the public realm around which future enriching layers of identity accumulate.

We seek to disseminate the learning through a variety of modes. This book is one such route, as are learning events and our initiative to link cities to the academic and research capability in the field of urbanism – entitled UniverCities.

Our aim is to progress the debate, learning, understanding and practice of urbanism through informed discourse. Our hope is to help transform the places of today to make them more sustainable and better-loved places of tomorrow.

This means providing a template of research and teaching that is enduring, something that can have a lasting value for the practitioners, creators and communities of tomorrow.

We hope you will enjoy this, the initial contribution to the debate by The Academy of Urbanism.

Reference

1 Tibbalds, Francis, *Making People-friendly Towns,* Spon Press, 2000

Jonathan Meades

Space? Place? Life?

Place – on no matter what scale – is one thing. Creation of place is quite another. That creation is accretive and continuous, it occurs across time. It is liable to owe as much to serendipitous juxtapositions and to malign interventions as it is to wilful design.

The interests of those who use place – that's every one of us – are not necessarily coincident with the interests of those who initially make place, those who set out the armature upon which subsequent generations will impose layers determined by utility, by successive technologies, by economic fluctuations and by fashion. Never underestimate the power of fashion, or collective taste.

It is today fashionable to tear down 1960s buildings, the good as well as the mediocre, just as in the 1960s it was fashionable to tear down Victorian buildings whose loss we now rue. The layers that survive the attentions of the demolition community will be amended by yet further generations, or stripped away and then replaced.

Every place we ever make carries the germ of its future archaeological dissection. That is an inevitability. So making places or buildings which are provisional, which shout about the possibility of flexibility, which proclaim their willingness to incorporate change, is redundant – and a sort of prospective vanity. They *will* change whether those initial makers like it or not, whether they make allowance for change or not. There are also future wars, imponderable climatic shifts and unforeseeable accidents to take into account. Place can only be made for the present and even then the reaction of the user, the spectator, can confound or disappoint the maker's expectations.

The only sort of place which allows the maker the satisfaction of knowing that it will mean what it is intended to mean is that which is pedagogic, a mental cage: the religious structure, including the arenas of totalitarian regimes and immense monuments that living gods erect to themselves. And these of course, after their thankfully brief period of utility, will be sacked, burnt, destroyed or employed by a contrary programme of mumbo-jumbo – mosques become churches, churches become mosques, the Third Reich's congress hall in Nuremberg became a pound for wrecked, stolen cars – strength through joyriding.

The Powers of Place: Hagia Sofia and the Blue Mosque, Istanbul.

This user (a word that makes place sound like a drug, and so it is) suffers a discomfiting sensation otherwise unknown to him when he surveys 'Le Grand Bleu' in Marseille, the law courts in Bordeaux, the Millau viaduct – a swelling of base national pride which is otherwise alien or at least buried. This is obviously not what the Lords Rogers and Foster and plain Mister Alsop intended when they made these structures – which happened, through their sheer potency, to have made places. This, I assure you, was not what I intended either.

I was shocked by the way that my inner aesthete was subjugated by my inner lout who presumably wants to put HP Sauce on cassoulet, wrap himself in the flag of St George and bellow about 'Ingerland ... land'. It merely goes to show that place is never pure, never simple, never predictable, even when place is new and yet unamended. Our compact with place is corrupted even before we set eyes on it.

It was always corrupted by expectation and anticipation, by the tales of men back from sea, by the promise of towers that reached to the clouds and the big rock candy mountain. It was increasingly corrupted by the democratisation of reproductions – steel prints, oleographs, Stevengraphs, photographs – the democratisation of print and mass literacy.

Place is today invariably popularly mediated, the distant is familiar. There is nowhere in the world we can go without having experienced an ocular clue to it. And an aural clue: we have heard the language and the music. And a gustatory, olfactory clue: we have tasted the food, we have sniffed it – in Headingley or Redlands, Haringey or Sparkbrook. Well ... a version of the food. Today we all arrive, semi-prepared by the virtual and with unprecedentedly greedy access to the actual. This may not be the fate of our grandchildren.

The Potency of Place: The Turning Torso, Malmö (Santiago Calatrava).

We are very likely living in an era when the world has achieved maximum shrinkage, and is smaller than it will be for a long time to come. The vanguards of this consequent insularity are already apparent, already domestically prescient: we are conscious of the depredations occasioned by promiscuous air travel and car travel; we know that much of the world which we still have the means to reach within hours comprises 'no-go' states. We are not going to be getaway people forever. Escape may not be an option.

We are consequently rediscovering our backyard; we are beginning to cherish it, if only in a *faute de mieux*-ish way. The signs are there. They may be tiny but they are telling. The allotment movement is thriving. The English seaside resort is at last being seen as having the potential to be something other than linear trash. There is a now almost conventionalised literature of inward travel, of sentient response to the immediately local, rather fancifully styled psycho-geography, which uncovers the latent exoticism of the everyday and the overlooked. This literature does what all literature does but without the encumbrances of plot and character. It invests place with mythology, with symbolism, with a kind of magic.

Its preferred, almost invariable subjects are edgelands where underfed horses freeze between interchanges and reservoirs, sewage outfalls, trails of rusty dereliction: but in its treatment of them it is within an ancient tradition of response to place, of reverence for place as the measure of our short life, and the trigger of nostalgia – just as the pastoral poets of the 18th and early 19th centuries were nostalgic for a wilder land not yet taken over by agriculture, not yet enclosed by the hedges that were perceived as industrial intruders. The London Dickens wrote of was a fantastical London of his childhood. Hardy's Dorset was an invention based as much on local newspaper stories from before he was born as on his extreme sensitivity to the places around him once he had moved back there to the house he designed: thank God that he designed nothing else.

I have to admit to a fondness for pitted former rolling stock dumped in fields, and for abandoned filling stations. But man cannot live by oxidisation alone. It's not a question of *either* atmospheric scrappiness *or* gleaming newbuild. It's a question of *both/and*. It's a

The Antithesis of Place:
almost anywhere on
the edge.

matter of the quality of the atmospheric scrappiness, the quality of the newbuild. Any place is better than the place which invites no response, which breeds indifference. The greatest offence in the creation of place is to attempt to avoid giving offence.

Without doubt the loudest, most widespread sign of our revived localism, our revived sensibility to place, is the manifestation of an appetite for that place called the inner city – which can be extended to include the inner town. And it is inevitable that our now-pristine inner cities of Corten steel – which is rebranded rust – of glass and pigmented concrete, of buildings shaped like pyrites and of bars serving climatically appropriate Mediterranean food will, in their turn, become the subjects of nostalgic reverie and satirical derision.

It goes without saying that the 20th century in Britain and in North America – though not really in Scotland and certainly not in much of Europe – was the century of *sub*urbia. The history of 20th-century urbanism in Britain is largely a history of a resistance to urbanism. And that resistance has not yet abated. We are constantly enjoined to believe that the future is sprawl and that we should, if not welcome it, just lie back and accede to it. That, very likely, is an old-fashioned future. It is of course a projection of the present. There exists a tendency to move beyond the resigned acceptance of sprawl as an unavoidable fact of life towards, first, passive toleration, and thence to a celebratory sanctioning of it.

Now, I'm all for perversity. But this is above and beyond. It's an alarmingly irresponsible route to pursue. The application of libertarian laissez-faire to the construction of new places or the alteration of old ones is grotesquely short-term. We should not believe in the sanctity of the free market when that market

When is rust not rust? When it's rebranded to the power of Corten. Community Youth Building, Begur, Catalonia.

affects place. To do so is to legitimise a return to the deregulation of the 1930s and ribbon development, to an era before town and country planning legislation, before the establishment of the currently threatened greenbelt.

It is not cooling towers and wind turbines that desecrate Britain's landscape but pseudo-Victorian hutches and neo-vernacular closes stranded in infrastructural limbo. It may be ideologically attractive to a certain cast of mind to grant licence to a volume builders' free-for-all but it will cause environmental mayhem of the most insipid kind. It guarantees a contaminated future. The lesson of the 20th century is surely very simple: it is not to follow its example, but rather to consider the legacy of place that we bequeath.

The buildings, the streets, the squares, which can do no more than provide the mere armature of place, are not consumer goods. Yet the most cursory scrutiny of Britain's constructional practice suggests that they are, in certain quarters, regarded thus. Magazines that reflect and flatter and special-plead on behalf of the professions and trades involved in construction suggest the same. My scrutiny of both happens to be far from cursory. Here's a list of places: Beverley, Bilbao, Chatham, Christchurch, Hornsey, Hull, Leeds, Letchworth, Liverpool, Manchester, Paris, Salisbury, Sherborne, Southwark, Spurn Head, Stowe, Le Vesinet, Winchester.

This is a very partial list of where I have filmed this year in the hope of making sense – however oblique, however notional – of what makes place, how place makes us, why place-makers make or made the places they do, or did. It would be rash, not to say impertinent, to extract generalities from this topographical overload. But it would be a professional dereliction were I not to. Damned if I do, damned if I don't.

When I talk about the elemental components of place being regarded as consumer goods, what I intend to convey is a truism that is perhaps not obvious to what was once described to me, with no irony, as the lay public – the truism that construction is an industry which is compelled to produce not for the needs of clients, not for the needs of different gamuts of society, not for the needs of place, but to ensure its own survival. Construction is undertaken for the sake of construction, for self-interest. The industry's duty to itself – if duty is not too dignifying a word – is to keep manufacturing. There has to be a constant flow of product. And that product is qualitatively different to any other on earth. It demands space, which in a small, overpopulated country is evidently a finite resource. Yet there is a reluctance to recognise it as such. We acknowledge that fish and oil are running out but we continue blithely to exhaust the supply of space with piratical abandon.

And that abandon persistently results in *unter*-place, low-grade place. Arriving in London from virtually anywhere in the developed world, one is struck by the meanness and the grimness of the endless 'burbs', but also by the sheer profligacy of land use. Overpopulation ought to occasion high-density development. But that is far from the case. Britain's lack of communality is surely linked to its wasteful tradition of low density, to its craving for horizontal spread, to the fact that each one of us requires a broader *cordon sanitaire* around us than the people of other European nations. We are much more sensitive than anyone to the infringement of our personal space in public places. The way we cringe and have the word *sorry* perpetually on our lips are expressions of the desire for separateness, of the desire to *possess* space rather than to share it.

Product – that's to say built structures – is also *quantitatively* different. It cannot enjoy the diminution in size which afflicts many manufactured goods from cars

Unter-place: the 'burbs'.

to computers, because humans are not shrinking in size. Further, there are ever more of us. The demands on space and the necessity for controlled husbandry of it increase in direct proportion to our numbers. And such control will not be exercised so long as the government's advisory quangos are composed of members with a pecuniary interest in construction, so long as the executive of the day listens to well-meaning volume builders whose responsibility is to their shareholders, creditors and, maybe, employees. It's hardly a case of the lunatics taking over the asylum – but *quis custodiet* and all that.

I appreciate that I sound way behind the times. There no longer exists such a thing as a volume builder, any more than there exists such a thing as comprehensive redevelopment. Today every volume builder is an urban regenerator – and that cleft discernible above the low-slung waistband of a pair of jeans is urban regenerator's bum. We have rebranded. A new logo, a new name: Thames Gateway becomes Thames Parkway ... this is the greatest of our national talents, the one we're world leader in. PR, spin, the peddling of willingly accepted delusion. The Ingerland... is-going-to-win-

The Veracity of Place: St. Andrews.

University of Sheffield
Dept of Architecture

Hulme, Manchester.

the-World-Cup syndrome is like a virus afflicting every area of our life.

We should not, however, allow the wall of delusion and hype to obscure what is being beneficially achieved for those not in the business of making place, nor to obscure the probable ramifications of those achievements. The urban regeneration we are witnessing today is the successor to the piecemeal, ad hoc process that began in earnest 30 or more years ago, predominantly in London, with the reclamation of certain inner city slums by the young and arty bourgeoisie – the process that would be widely calumnised as gentrification. Why was it calumnised? Liberal self-hatred? Envy? It was the seed of an urban renaissance. It was both economically rooted – the house price differential was then skewed in the other direction – and culturally reactive to the magnet of the 'burbs' that had lured immediately previous generations.

What we are witnessing today is the second stage of that reclamation – gentrification through newbuild. Often visually impressive if somewhat homogenised newbuild: synthetic modernism or neo-modernism or pastiche modernism or populist modernism or accessible modernism. Whatever you like to call it, clearly there's a widespread taste for it. Especially among the affluent young – perhaps because they know nothing else. Private sector domestic building is achieving the level of quality that only the best public schemes achieved in the 30 years after the Second World War. And it will fare better because the self-interest of owner-occupiers is more entrenched than that of tenants. This is a way of suggesting that fate of place depends upon who uses and occupies place.

We're deluding ourselves – again – if we pretend that income and the wherewithal to buy is not as much a determinant of place as the recipes that social engineering once proffered. A proprietorial ethos counts for more than pedestrianisation, street furniture, lumps of sculpture, clever arborealism, etcetera. That etcetera includes the services – shops, restaurants and so on – which belong to the soufflé economy on which the oven door will one day be opened, the not very far-off day when foreclosure becomes a norm. When we look at, say, the centre of Leeds or innermost Manchester – and here we have to acknowledge the part played by such promoters of regeneration as Gerry Adams and Martin

Hulme, Manchester.

McGuinness – we see the future of English urbanism, a future which is both exhilarating and profoundly disturbing. It is a future which has mercifully shunned sprawl. Those cities and the other great formerly industrial cities, the virtual city-states of the north and Midlands, are now competing with each other as they did in the mid to late 19th century, the era of mighty civic buildings and municipal pomp. Today it is not a question of who has the grandest town hall – it was always Leeds – but of who builds highest, who has the flashiest landmark, who has the most bridges by Calatrava or someone plagiarising Calatrava.

Those landmarks have certainly worked their magic: it is directly due to them that there are no more drive-by shootings in Hulme, no more crack dens in Moss Side, no more bomb factories in Beeston. What we are actually witnessing is an abandonment of the North American model and an espousal of the French model. The embourgeoisement of the inner city combined with a dereliction in the matter of building social housing to replace that which was so carelessly sold off is effecting an economically enforced demographic shift. Social polarities are not going to disappear. The sites of income-defined ghettos are merely being exchanged. They're swapping with each other. A new hierarchy of place is being created. The *haves* move inwards. The *havenots* move, or are forced, outwards. There is a significant population who cannot afford the affordable. Privilege is centripetal. Want is centrifugal. It can be summed up like this: in the future, deprivation, crime and riots will be comfortably confined to outside the ring road. That is the pessimistic, dystopian, despairing prospectus. It need not be the only one.

It is no coincidence that the urbanism which is most widely revered is that of the 18th and early 19th centuries when there existed an explicit Enlightenment belief that place could promote happiness – a belief we have lost. The means by which such an ethos can begin to be regained are not complicated, but they are not vouchsafed either to place-makers or to users. They demand governmental will – a will to create a new framework. A will, such as exists in Spain, to discriminate positively against chain stores: they are forbidden to open for as many hours as small retailers who are not subjected to the same rate burden as the behemoths.

URBIS in the new Manchester: any more in the trophy cabinet?

The refurbishment of the Brunswick Centre in Bloomsbury is architecturally exemplary. Urbanistically, it is a disappointment because the quirky shops and galleries have been replaced by the same chains that we see everywhere else on our corporately inhabited high streets.

It *is* possible to legislate for quality of life and for equitable prosperity. Four-fifths of inward investment to Britain is to the south-east. The reason is simple. Our Third World transport scares off investors. Accessibility is a trigger of renewal: look at Marseille. We missed out on TGV: we are thus in a position to leapfrog a generation of technology and go straight to Maglev, which would put Manchester within 20 minutes of Birmingham, and Birmingham within half an hour of London. Such a rebalancing would take the heat off the south-east. This sounds like infrastructural utopianism. At a micro-level, just widening a pavement – and Britain's are notoriously narrow – is a device for returning civility to cities.

A notable proportion of the contenders for the Urbanism Awards are places which owe their specialness to the very fact that they are controlled. They are, all of them, atypical. But what is atypical in one era can, if we learn from it, if we seek to emulate it, become typical in the next – you know, tiny stream burgeons to become great river.

Christopher Balch

Cities: Continuity & Change

Dublin, Edinburgh & London

The shortlisting of Dublin, Edinburgh and London as candidates for The Academy of Urbanism's European City of the Year Award 2006 reflected their status as the most successful cities in these islands politically, economically and culturally. While other cities strive to improve their international competitiveness, these capitals occupy the dominant position in the urban culture of their respective countries of Ireland, Scotland and England.

Identifying the factors of success in Dublin, Edinburgh and London is necessarily a complex and challenging intellectual task. The Core Cities Programme[1] sought to identify the factors contributing to the economic competitiveness of European cities and concluded that the following are critical features:

- economic diversity
- skilled workforce
- connectivity – internal and external
- capacity to mobilise and implement long-term development strategies
- innovation in firms and organisations
- quality of life – social, cultural, environmental

There is no doubt that the success of cities depends, to a very great extent, on their ability to attract and retain the best people and businesses in an increasingly global marketplace. This is based on an essentially economic view of the function of cities[2].

The principles set out in The Academy of Urbanism's Manifesto seek to promote a wider and more holistic view of the combination of factors that are needed to promote high-quality urban areas and which prompt the following challenges for city leaders:

- Is the city well managed, inclusive, fair and well run?
- Does the city provide a unique and distinctive sense of place, identity and cultural resonance?
- Is the city an attractive, safe and enticing place for people to live, work, play, visit and enjoy?

View east along the Liffey.

View from Edinburgh Castle north towards the Forth.

View east along the River Thames.

Edinburgh Castle

☐ Does the city provide a conducive environment for the creation and distribution of wealth and is it able to support the maintenance and improvement of its urban environment?

☐ Does the city exhibit and promote environmentally sustainable behaviour and community cohesion?

☐ Does the city provide transport and access options to an appropriate range of urban services?

Dublin, Edinburgh and London provide examples of 'best practice' in many respects; however, the real challenge for cities is achieving a balance between frequently competing demands. For example, strong city leadership may occur at the expense of true community involvement and, similarly, a strong economy may threaten the distinctive qualities of place through the destruction of historic assets.

The challenge for cities is to maintain continuity while embracing the need for continuing physical, economic and social change. Successful urbanism requires constant reinvention based on a respect for space, place and life.

As great capital cities, Dublin, Edinburgh and London share strong similarities as well as distinct differences. It is no accident of history that all are sited alongside east-facing estuaries (of the Liffey, Forth and Thames), providing opportunities for defence, movement and, above all, trade with the wider world. From the security and repression exercised from the castles of Dublin and Edinburgh and the Tower of London grew governmental power, which today accounts for the presence of democratic and cultural institutions associated with a capital city function.

So these great waterfront communities developed, attracted by the opportunities to trade throughout the British Isles, Europe and increasingly further afield. The commodities shipped through Dublin, Edinburgh and London provided the raw materials for manufacturing and commerce. Today, the docklands of these three great cities provide much-needed land to accommodate new forms of economic activity and the populations which are growing to serve them – demonstrating continuity and change.

Above all, the confidence and outward-looking nature of these capital cities provide the seedbed for cultural development and the interchange of information and ideas. The growth of scientific thought focused on the Royal Society in London, the contribution of the Edinburgh Enlightenment to modern concepts of moral philosophy and political economy, and the blossoming of Irish literature bear witness to the environment which these cities have provided for creativity. This is reflected in the existence of world-class centres of learning and

research, such as Trinity College Dublin, Edinburgh University and the University of London, and their continuing success in attracting new talent.

Despite strong parallels in economic and social history in the three cities, there are marked contrasts in the evolution of urban form. The medieval city core is most marked in Edinburgh's Old Town, which straddles the geological 'crag and tail' formation running between the Castle and the Palace of Holyrood. The acute changes in level in the natural topography of the city encouraged a vertical dimension when developing the old 'fish-bone' plan of medieval Edinburgh that gave birth to the stone-built tenement as a distinctive Scottish architectural form and encouraged a tradition of high-density urban living more European than British.

The permanence of stone as a building material stands in contrast to the vulnerability of Dublin

Big Ben.

Dublin Castle.

Figure Ground Plan Dublin

A LILT FOR DUBLIN

I talk. You talk. We talk. The words
Somehow hang in the air and turn
Like memories turn and ideas turn
And gradually the talk makes a city.

I walk. You walk. We walk. The walk
Takes us over the river and through the streets
That are living streets and singing streets
And slowly the walk makes a city.

I look. You sit. I laugh. You point
Out the view from Stephen's Green
And the trees are green and the talk is green
And the look and the walk and the streets
And the laugh and the point and the ideas
And the sit and the memories
Make a city.

Temple Bar by night.

and London's wooden buildings, which fell prey to the twin ravages of fire and urban redevelopment. However, the distinctive characters of Temple Bar and the City of London bear witness to the cities' essentially medieval street patterns, despite the pressures to accommodate new economic activities.

For all three cities, however, their emergence into the 'modern world' drew together the classical revival of the Renaissance, the ideas of rationalism, growing wealth from colonial trade and the world's first Industrial Revolution. The physical manifestation of this was the order and unity of the Georgian city: Bloomsbury, Soho, Mayfair and the Nash terraces of London; Merrion Square, the colleges and greens south of the Liffey in Dublin; and the formal Presbyterian order of James Craig's plan for Edinburgh's New Town. In Edinburgh Georgian development was brought about by civic endeavour – the result of a unified attitude towards life, the unified ownership of land and the unified control of the architect and builder.

In Dublin, the Wide Streets Commission swept away medieval streets to create fashionable squares and terraces for Dublin's ruling and merchant classes, while in London speculation and development of the landed estates to the north and west of the City created the elegance of Bloomsbury, Mayfair and Belgravia.

The Georgian components of Dublin, Edinburgh and London today remain largely intact and are the subject of strict conservation controls. While this limits the scope for physical change, it ensures continuity in the urban fabric and provides clear evidence of the attractiveness of high-density urban living close to the city core. Indeed, the hearts of these three great cities are essentially a combination of medieval and Georgian urban form.

The 19th century brought rapid growth and expansion to British cities and, while Dublin, Edinburgh and London may have avoided the worst consequences of industrialisation seen

Below: Scottish tenement buildings. High-rise living – medieval style.

Right: Tenement Close, Edinburgh.

Bottom: London city skyline.

elsewhere, conditions for the urban poor remained squalid. However, concerns for public health led to the development of municipal government and a gradual process of improvement to living conditions in the city. But, for many, the answer lay in escape to newly developed suburbs made accessible by growing rail and tram networks.

The process of suburbanisation continued apace in all three cities throughout the 20th century, facilitated by the individual freedom conferred by the car. While there is a growing recognition that the combined effect of individual freedoms may be tyranny in terms of congestion and pollution of the core, the centrifugal forces acting on Dublin,

Edinburgh and London remain intense. While the populations of the three cities are growing, they continue to lose people to surrounding areas, driven by the shortage of attractive and affordable housing.

For all three cities, the challenge is how to deliver economic growth and increased residential population within their boundaries. The focus is therefore firmly upon the reuse of derelict, dismissed or contaminated land and the provision of new commercial accommodation. How this is achieved will have a marked impact on the future of these cities for succeeding generations. In the same way that planned development in the 18th century created places which we now seek to conserve, so the creation of new urban quarters for the 21st century presents opportunities for a new urbanism.

In Dublin and London the river that bisects the city has been the focus for an extraordinary physical and cultural revival. The creation of riverside walkways and investment in new bridges have reconnected the river with residents and visitors alike, and provide a backdrop for the creative reuse of old industrial buildings. This is exemplified by the conversion of the former Bankside Power Station into Tate Modern and the creation of the new iconic 'London Eye'. These developments have acted as catalysts for the resurgence of the South Bank as a vibrant, mixed-use quarter of the city, albeit in a somewhat unplanned and haphazard fashion, retaining the best of the old and developing striking new buildings.

This stands in contrast to the redevelopment of much of the docklands of Dublin and London, where the pressure to create modern accommodation for banking and financial services companies attracted by tax incentives has led to new urban structures that owe little to the form or character of the cities or communities where they are located. While Dublin's International Financial Services Centre and London's Canary Wharf have undoubtedly added to the economic success of these cities, they do not stand scrutiny in terms of the Principles of Urbanism.

The City of London and Edinburgh's Financial District provide more instructive case studies of how modern commercial accommodation can be integrated into sensitive locations through attention to the existing urban grain and ground-level environment. Fitting in the large ground floors required by commercial occupiers poses substantial challenges in terms of building scale and mass. However, as Paternoster Square and the Edinburgh Exchange demonstrate, new development that meets the needs of modern business and provides an appropriate and elegant form can be successfully introduced into historic city cores.

Three current projects serve to show the energy and determination required to deliver large-scale regeneration that will produce lasting benefits for present and future communities.

A LONG SENTENCE FOR EDINBURGH …

This is a city where history
Layers on history and stone
Layers on stone and walking
Breeds walking down a narrow close
Into a vista that makes you gasp
As vista piles on vista and the trains
Pull into Waverley and vista piles
On history piles on stone piles
On stories piles on legends piles
On Old Town piles on New Town
On a city built on history

And ready for tomorrow.

Figure Ground Plan Edinburgh

Ballymun in north Dublin has been the focus of a concerted effort to regenerate community housing in a high-rise estate on the edge of the city. Conceived in the early 1960s as a project to re-house the occupants of squalid inner city tenements, the scheme adopted system-building techniques to create over 3,000 new dwellings. By the end of the decade, a new community had been created without the amenities necessary for everyday living. Growing unpopularity led to the estate becoming home to a large unemployed and transient population. By the early 1990s, community activists and Dublin Corporation recognised the need for radical action. Ballymun Regeneration Ltd was established in 1997 to facilitate community consultation and develop and implement a masterplan for regeneration.

Unpopular tower blocks have been demolished and a new mixed-use community is beginning to emerge as Ballymun becomes a place popular to live in. The community is built around a new town centre and distinct neighbourhoods offering a mix of housing types. Ballymun is an object lesson for all cities. Regeneration needs to address the physical, economic and social needs of communities and cannot be successfully delivered without effective consultation.

Top Left: Halfpenny Bridge Dublin

Top Right: Hungerford Bridge London

A Georgian Door Dublin

The waterfront presents Edinburgh with the opportunity to create a new series of urban quarters less than 3 kilometres from the city centre, on land which was previously used for industry and related port activities. Plans have been developed for three distinct areas of development at Granton, Western Harbour and Leith Docks, based on a mix of new housing, job opportunities and new community assets serving both existing and new populations. Proposals are well advanced for a new tram route providing links along the waterfront and to the city centre.

Left Top: Dublin Financial Centre.
Left Middle: Old and new buildings in Edinburgh.
Left Botton: Ballymun new housing.
Below: Ballymun 1960s high-rise.

incorporating historic buildings to provide an extensive mixed-use development supporting 25,000 jobs and nearly 2,000 homes.

Conceived as a dense, vibrant and distinctive urban quarter, the development will comprise adaptable urban blocks set within a framework of key routes and spaces. Nearly half of the main site will be made up of new public areas including twenty new streets and ten new public spaces. By applying upper and lower limits on different uses and building heights across the site, the plan establishes the density and scale of development. This will be subject to design guidelines governing matters such as building techniques, and materials and how they will be used.

In many respects, the plans for King's Cross can be seen as a 21st-century response to the same challenge of making attractive urban districts that faced Craig, Adam and Woods in the 18th century. While diversity is the norm in today's society, there is still a need for a unified ownership and control to deliver a lasting urban vision.

At the city level, vision requires both strong leadership and a clear sense of purpose. This is evident in all three cities. Dublin City Council has adopted a clear development strategy which responds to the Irish government's National Spatial Strategy and Regional Planning Guidelines for the

A range of public and private sector bodies are involved in bringing about a long-term transformation in the city that is largely market-led, although guided by a series of development frameworks and masterplans. It is not immediately apparent from these or from the built form that is now emerging how a unique and strong sense of place and cultural identity will be achieved. A new waterfront city may be the result but it remains to be seen whether or not it will be distinctively Edinburgh.

At King's Cross in London, after nearly six years of work, plans are underway to regenerate the land between St Pancras and King's Cross stations,

Forth shore, Bottom: Shoppers on Grafton Street.

Greater Dublin Area. The vision is to make Dublin a leading European city and enhance the quality of life and experience for the residents, workers, commuters and visitors. The plan is to consolidate the urban form of the city in conjunction with improvements to the public transport network. Expansion and intensification of the city centre is planned to reinforce, strengthen and protect its civic design, character and dignity. The key to success will be delivering continued improvements to public transport, to serve a city whose citizens retain a strong attachment to their cars.

Edinburgh City Council is promoting long-term strategic thinking about the future scale and direction of the city, which is seen as a leading Northern European capital that continues to drive its regional and national economy. In a recent consultation document, 'Vision for Capital Growth', the City Council sets out its ideas for a prosperous, connected city whose long-term growth is guided by a shared understanding of future city form. The vision is based on radial development centred on public transport routes, a network of strategic green wedges and new mechanisms for delivering the necessary infrastructure. At the heart of the suggested strategy is a commitment to supporting the city's centre and protecting its superb built and natural heritage.

The election of a Mayor for London in 2000 gave new impetus to planning at a city-wide level. The London Plan sets out a clear strategy for accommodating growth of population and jobs in sustainable patterns of development based on an improved and expanded public transport network.

Flower stalls, London, Below: Street performer in Grafton Street, Dublin

Mayor Ken Livingstone was clear that London had to become a more densely populated, intensively used city, and at the same time more open, accessible and better designed. Development has been directed towards areas of social and economic deprivation, derelict or disused sites, areas of historical neglect and future opportunities. This is epitomised by plans for areas such as Stratford, where the 2012 Olympics is expected to provide the catalyst for the regeneration of East London.

Across all three cities, the delivery of ambitious plans for growth and renewal within an established, historical urban fabric presents huge challenges, particularly for London where the sheer scale and complexity of managing a 'World City' is compounded by two tiers of local government. By contrast, Dublin and Edinburgh are fortunate to be of a scale where the gulf between strategic policy-making and sensitivity to local interests is for the most part bridgeable.

For all three cities, however, it is apparent that enabling and encouraging people to use sustainable forms of transport is a key priority. This requires long-term investment and an integrated approach to land use and transport planning to produce a user-friendly, more car-free environment. There are encouraging signs of what can be achieved, but much remains to be done if these cities are to achieve the quality of pedestrian environment enjoyed by many European capitals, as exemplified by Copenhagen, voted the RIBA European City of the Year in 2005.

Figure Ground Plan London

LONDON

If my task today is to try to squeeze
London into these few urban lines
I'll have to think of all the languages
That sing in this city from across the map;
That whisper like a stream, gush like a tap.

This is a city built on sentences,
On arguments and on reflections,
On points of view and intersections
Imagined and real: high rises of the soul
With train line, palace, office block, school

Park, theatre, bus stop, river
An A to Z that goes on for ever.

Princes Street Gardens

Edinburgh comes closest to achieving this. It is a great city to walk through. Its urban core is compact and easy to read, and its streets are lively and usable. This is a reflection of the high-density urban living of tenements and Georgian urban form that supports a wide variety of uses. In addition, Edinburgh provides enormous richness in the parks and open spaces it offers to residents and visitors alike.

Dublin is making steady advances in improving conditions for its pedestrians. Fully pedestrianised streets such as Grafton Street and Henry Street throng with people, while the walking environment alongside the River Liffey and in O'Connell Street has been transformed. However, much of the city centre remains dominated by road traffic.

The introduction of congestion charging in London has significantly reduced the level of city-centre traffic. This has allowed more space to be created

for pedestrians in locations such as Trafalgar Square. Further schemes were introduced through the Mayor's 100 Public Spaces programme. However, much of London remains dominated and degraded by traffic and suffers from the absence of a high-quality pedestrian network.

Do cities exist as single entities rather than an assemblage of places? Certainly for metropolitan cities such as London it is hard to define a unifying sense of place other than in parts of the city core, along the River Thames or through a collection of iconic buildings. Perhaps more than anything, the hallmark of London is its sheer scale and diversity – physically, economically and culturally. The scale of Edinburgh and Dublin makes the search for local character and distinctiveness less elusive. Certainly Edinburgh's heroic geology and landscape give it a unique and recognisable signature. Perhaps more than anything else the character of a city lies in its people and culture.

Liffey Walkway, Bottom: Walkway through Dublin Park

Above all, cities are places for living in. Whether viewed from an economic, community or physical perspective, successful cities such as Dublin, Edinburgh and London must both meet the needs of their population and inspire human endeavour and civilisation. In short, they need to provide the qualities of good urbanism in order to flourish.

References
1 Office of the Deputy Prime Minister, *Competitive European Cities – Where Do the Core Cities Stand?*, January 2004.
2 Mumford, Lewis, *The City in History*, Secker & Warburg, 1961.

London Street market.
Edinburgh topography.
Trafalgar Square.

David Rudlin

Learning from towns

Ludlow, Lincoln & St. Ives

There is something extraordinary about a successful town. It has an energy and a sense of community and purpose not found anywhere else – small enough for many of its people to know each other, but large enough to provide the shops, facilities and public institutions that make it a special place.

The three towns shortlisted for the first Academy of Urbanism's Great Town Award are all excellent, if very different, examples of this phenomenon. They include two small towns, Ludlow and St. Ives, which have been successful in reinventing themselves over the last ten years and one large town, Lincoln – with more than eight times their population – which is more a small city. The Academy of Urbanism visited each of these towns and spent time talking to a wide range of people. We walked their streets to fathom just what it is that makes the towns special and what they were doing to create or preserve this 'specialness'.

What is a town?

The word 'town' has developed two subtly different meanings that together convey a town's unique character. The first is almost an English equivalent of the word 'urban' – so you can have 'town centre' or a 'town house', you can 'go to town', be a 'man about town' or 'paint the town red'. These terms relate to the bright lights of the town as seen from the country – Borchester as seen from fictional Ambridge. However, 'town' also implies smallness and parochialism; this is the town viewed from the city, the place from which every red-blooded youth yearns to escape.

Being a town is partly about size, it has something to do with a separate identity (Hammersmith, for example, is not a town) and it also has an administrative dimension as epitomised by that most British of institutions, the Town Council. From the perspective of

Above: The Streets of Ludlow have been the focus of community life for centuries.

Above Right: The Streets of St. Ives throng with life throughout the year.

Right: Lincoln is as big as many small cities but retains many town characteristics.

Towns like Ludlow cater for the commercial, professional and spiritual needs of their people.

The Academy of Urbanism, a town is probably the smallest form of settlement in which true urbanism can exist.

The Great Towns category is therefore very wide, including places like Ludlow and St. Ives alongside the much larger Lincoln. Home to 86,000 people and a service centre for twice that number, Lincoln is really a city. However, because of its character, history and administration it has the soul of a town, something that could not be said, for example, of Coventry, Sunderland and Bradford, which may not be much larger.

Lincoln, the oldest of these three 'Great Towns', was founded in AD 48 as a Roman fort to pacify the surrounding countryside. Ludlow's history began with the development of the castle in 1086 while St. Ives developed as a fishing village on a sand spit – not the sort of event for which records are kept.

Since their foundation, the prosperity of all three towns has waxed and waned. In the 5th to 9th centuries, Lincoln was virtually abandoned, but by the time of the Domesday Book it had grown into a city a third of the size of London. Yet by the 16th century it was once more in steep decline with a population of just 2,500. In late medieval times, Ludlow housed the Council of the Marches which ruled over Wales and the Borders. St. Ives' heyday came in the 19th century when its port was at its height and the arrival of the railway made it a visitor destination.

There are common threads that run through these histories. Each of the three towns has acted as a local service centre for its surrounding hinterland, providing a market for goods, a centre for professional services such as doctors and solicitors and specialist trades, a social, spiritual and political hub, and an administrative and political centre. However, each has prospered when it has managed to supplement this

Lincoln's siting on a steep escarpment preserved the old town from redevelopment.

day-to-day activity with a speciality, something that it can 'sell' to a much wider market, be it St. Ives' salted herring or Lincoln's religious guidance.

Two periods shaped the character of British towns – the Industrial Revolution, when the urbanisation of rural populations smothered many towns, and the post-war period of redevelopment, modernism and road building that came to a head in the late 1960s and did untold damage to many towns.

Lincoln, with a thousand years of civic government, grew from 7,000 to more than 50,000 inhabitants in the 19th century, and still bears the scars of this growth. What saved it from the fate of other towns swallowed up by the Industrial Revolution or replanned in the 1960s was the topography of the old town, which was too steep for redevelopment, and the strength of institutions such as the cathe-

dral. As a result, it developed outside its town walls, much as happened in many of the finest Italian towns. This area was the focus of activity for 1960s planners and this is still evident today.

St. Ives and Ludlow were also saved from these twin threats, partly because of their isolation. While both towns had their industries, be it tin or the port in St. Ives, or gloves in Ludlow, the conditions were not right for the sort of population growth that occurred in other towns. Ludlow became something of a backwater while St. Ives developed as a resort. In both cases, they retained their historic buildings and street patterns. Both towns also escaped the 1960s because there was neither the demand nor the opportunity to build civic precincts, shopping centres or ring roads. There is surely no greater indictment of modern town planning than the extent to which we value its absence.

The successful town like St. Ives is not the one that attracts outsiders, it's the one that survives them with its character intact.

The challenges

For years, in our imaginations at least, towns have provided a stable backdrop to the turmoil of the cities, havens of tranquillity and prosperity, the very epitome of Middle England. Times are changing, however. Towns can no longer rely on the provision of services to their agricultural hinterland as the 'baseload' of their economy. Farming has become a global business, dealing directly with supermarkets, while people living in rural hinterlands are increasingly mobile and, if their local town no longer appeals, it is only another 20 minutes in the Range Rover to the next town or twice that into the city. At the same time, the industries of small towns such as brewing, food processing and engineering are being absorbed into multi-national businesses without local connections or loyalties.

Lincoln, Ludlow and St. Ives illustrate a different set of challenges. They have lost traditional industries but not suffered from dramatic population decline and economic stagnation. Like many pretty towns, particularly those with good road and rail connections, they have become commuter centres. Where commuting is difficult they have become weekend retreats, filling up with second homes and holiday cottages, or retirement centres for people selling up and moving out of the cities.

These trends present both opportunities and challenges. Ludlow, Lincoln and St. Ives are great towns because they have exploited the opportunities and confronted the challenges. In each case, the key has been to make the most of the money and energy of incomers – be they residents in Ludlow, tourists in St. Ives or students in Lincoln – without losing their authenticity or what makes them special. Each of the three tells a story of transformation that offers lessons for other towns facing similar challenges.

LUDLOW

'The most perfect town in England'
Betjeman said, and he should know.
He had an eye and an ear for England;
For English light, for that English glow
As the River Teme and a Shropshire sky
Combine in a perfect Ludlow way
And as the sun goes down and the night clouds fly
You can wallow at the end of a Ludlow day
In Ludlow Sausage and Ludlow Cheese
And a pint of a perfect local beer
And the sound of laughter carried on the breeze
From people just happy that they're here.
From the Castle down to Old Street, Ludlow is the place
To put heaven in your belly and a smile upon your face!

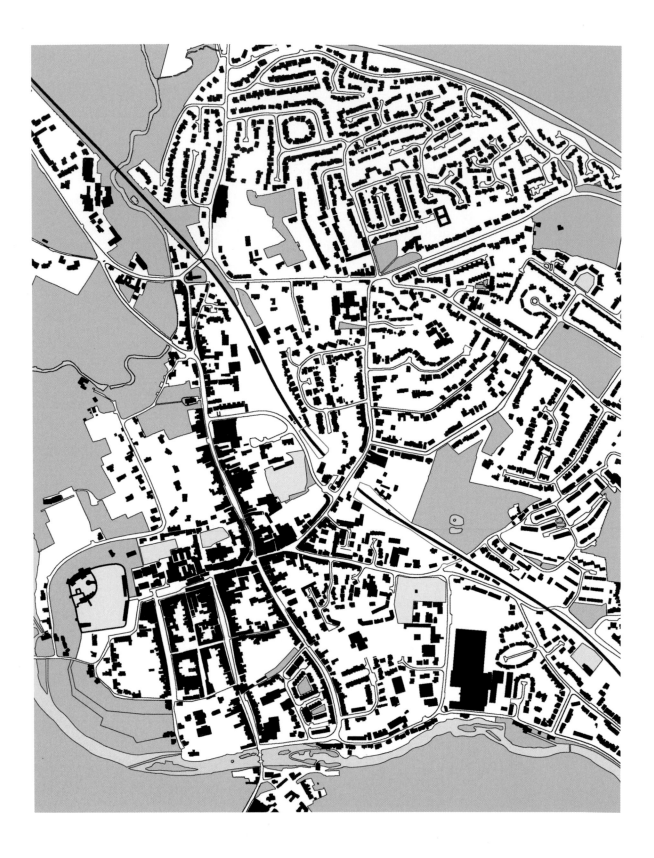

Left: Figure ground: Ludlow. Below: Aerial photo of Ludlow.

Ludlow

For anyone looking for the iconic English town, Ludlow is almost too good to be true. It was described by John Betjeman as 'probably the loveliest town in England', a view shared by the hundreds of barristers, doctors and other professional people who have moved there in recent years. Ludlow is a perfectly preserved town full of traditional independent businesses operating out of historic half-timbered buildings, and run by an engaged and committed local community.

However, as recently as ten years ago the town was tatty and run down. It was seen as too remote to attract incomers and was suffering from the decline of local agriculture. Its fine stock of historic buildings survived largely because, for the last few centuries,

values have been insufficient to justify redevelopment. Its independent traders, likewise, have been insulated by the lack of interest shown in the town by national retail chains.

Since then, Ludlow has been transformed. It is now bustling with life, the shops are thriving and investment has seen many of the buildings sympathetically refurbished. Its achievement has been to embrace change without becoming part of what Mark Lynas called the 'march of the clone towns'.[1] It has retained its distinctive character and, most important, the sense of community and belonging that binds it together. It is no coincidence that Ludlow is the first British town to become a member of the international 'Cittaslow' movement, started

Below: Ludlow market place at the gates of the castle (below)

Right: Most of Ludlow's shops remain occupied by independent retailers. This is at the heart of the town's appeal

by Italian cities seeking to preserve these traditional town characteristics in an ever-accelerating world.

Ludlow has a population of around 10,000 people and is therefore very different to larger places like Lincoln. People born and brought up there probably went to the same secondary school and tend to know each other, regardless of status. This is reflected in a willingness to get involved in running the town through the Town Council and numerous local trusts. The incomers are also a formidable bunch, bringing with them professional expertise and organisational ability. This is a powerful resource when mixed with the commitment of the long-term community who seem to have accepted these incomers.

When something needs fixing in Ludlow – be it repairing the town walls, sorting out the weirs on the river or combating anti-social behaviour in the churchyard – a trust is formed at a public meeting and people get on with raising money (over £1 million in the case of the weirs). This 'can-do' attitude is what has allowed Ludlow to survive its renaissance.

The influx of affluent people also has negative aspects. It has pushed up house prices beyond the reach of many local people and taken Ludlow upmarket, making it more middle class with a focus on quality of service and quality of life. However, the town has avoided the artificiality of chic boutiques and wine bars often associated with this type of gentrification. One of the reasons is the way that it has embraced the 'Slow Food' and 'Cittaslow' movements, which focus on traditional ways of life, service and food, and manages to unite local communities, traditional shops and businesses with incomers attracted by the way of life that they represent.

The Ludlow food and drink festival is an important part of the town's calendar. The focus on food helps to support many of the town's independent retailers.

Ludlow has avoided the chic boutiques and wine bars found in other affluent towns.

Left: Figure ground: Lincoln, Below: Aerial photo of Lincoln.

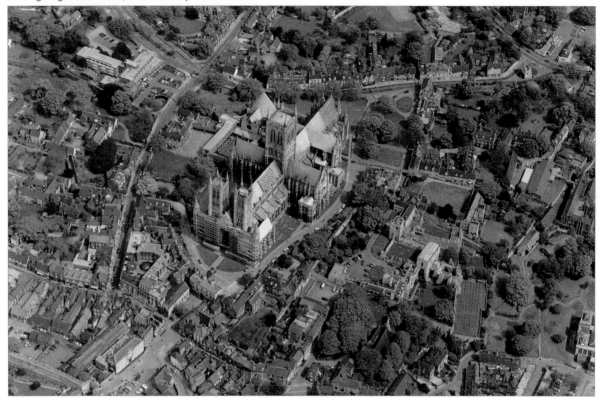

Lincoln

The slogan coined for Lincoln's 2020 vision was 'one of the world's great small cities'. It also has 'city' problems – congestion, unsympathetic developments from the 1960s and 1970s, and the closure of traditional industries. However, as in Ludlow, there is a strong tradition of civic involvement and partnership, with the town's 'movers and shakers' all knowing each other. Lincoln's partnerships are not, like those of Ludlow, born out of public meetings, but regeneration partnerships spending public money, with the same sense of purpose and collaboration. What Lincoln could reasonably claim to have is the best of both worlds: the buzz of a city and the intimacy and fellowship of a town.

In physical terms, Lincoln is a town of two halves. The historic old town – clinging to the slopes of an escarpment, on top of which sit the castle and cathedral – retains one of its Roman gates and still has the character of an historic citadel; the top of

the hill between the castle and the cathedral is one of the great public spaces in England. The other Lincoln lies outside its historic city walls, growing outwards in the 19th century. It is an area that retains some Victorian buildings but which has also been thoroughly knocked about by post-war planners and now looks like many British cities, dominated by unsympathetic buildings, ring roads and large-format retailing. This is the area where the greatest transformation is taking place.

Despite its great history, Lincoln does not quite have the appeal of York or Chester and lacks the catchment population of larger cities. Until recently, it was a relatively poor town and, like Ludlow, rather shabby and run down. Lincoln's great success has been the way that it has turned around its fortunes. There are many elements to this including the development of tourism and the promotion of quality food, events and festivals through the 'Tastes of

LINCOLN

You see the Cathedral first as you drive into the city
And words fail you; your mouth becomes an O
And what can you say ? It's not nice, it's not pretty,
It's bigger words than that, words that sing more.

Then the calf-stretching walk up Steep Hill to the top
And words fail again; I should get out my pad
And draw these delights as my jaw starts to drop
And descriptive words die in the void in my head.

Should I dance it, or sculpt my response to this place ?
This city, you see, is a true work of art
An ecstatic effusion of stone, light and space
That nurtures the soul, and transplants the heart.

Lincoln

Lincoln University will soon have 10,000 students and is probably the most important element of the town's regeneration.

The Guildhall in Lincoln: for centuries the town's guilds met here to govern the town.

Lincolnshire' campaign. This brings together the same potent forces as the 'Cittaslow' movement, supporting local producers, projecting an authentic image while promoting quality of life. The emphasis on quality of life is attracting both visitors and residents, and Lincoln is able to take advantage of this through substantial new housing development. A major urban extension is being developed – the Western Growth Corridor – with 4,500 new homes planned through an 'Enquiry by Design' process by the Prince's Foundation.

Perhaps the most important group of new residents in Lincoln is its students. At the heart of the town's regeneration is the development of the university that opened in 1996 but now feels like it has always been there. The campus, which will soon be home to 10,000 students, is being developed on a former railway site in the heart of Lincoln and is transforming both the economy and the appearance of the town. As other cities have found, universities are engines of economic growth, not only because of spin-offs in research and development, but because they attract talented people who forever retain an attachment to the place.

Lincoln is therefore a combination of tradition and modernism, something that is reflected in its attitude to the built environment. Its work in this area is being used as a national pilot by English Heritage and involves a comprehensive database of urban archaeology, an assessment of what is significant, and conservation plans for key buildings. However, respect for the past does not mean that new buildings are required to be historical pastiche. Lincoln is developing a fine collection of contemporary buildings including the museum (The Collection) by Panter Hudspith, the Cultural Industries building by Bauman Lyons, and the new university campus with various architects, including a school of architecture by Rick Mather.

The revival of the fishing industry is an extraordinary success and adds to the town's authenticity. Right: Figure ground: St. Ives.

St. Ives

The youngest of the three towns, St. Ives grew up as a fishing village on a beach. Its people used to have to walk two hours to Hayle to worship and so resolved in the 15th century to build their own parish church, to save the walk. This spirit of communal effort is still very much part of the town.

St. Ives was once so remote that its cultural links were with Wales, Ireland, France and Spain rather than the rest of England. This situation was transformed by the arrival of the railway in the mid 19th century, after which the town developed rapidly as a resort. Some of the earliest visitors were artists such as Turner and writers such as Virginia Woolf, followed later in the 1950s by Barbara Hepworth, Ben Nicholson and Patrick Heron. As a resort, it has never become unfashionable or fallen into decline. Its achievement has been to survive its popularity without losing its spirit by becoming either a 'kiss-me-quick' seaside town or a playground of the rich. As one resident put it: "St. Ives is a great place to visit because it is a great place to live." The emphasis is on serving local people and concentrating on quality of life rather than pandering to the whims of visitors.

The town is full of studios and galleries, but the modern symbol of this artistic heritage is the Tate, opened in 1993 as the first branch of the gallery to be built outside London and now one of Cornwall's three year-round tourist attractions (with Eden and the National Maritime Museum). The arts are important because they attract people wishing to browse the galleries but also because they project an upmarket image. The second factor behind the success of St. Ives is it's surf culture, which is manifest in trendy bars on the seafront, surf clothing shops and groups of tousled, tanned youths 'hanging out' in its streets and squares. It is this that makes the town 'cool' and attractive to young people, something that British resorts have struggled to achieve for years. The third factor, which is common to Ludlow and Lincoln, is the importance of food, reflected through restaurants, festivals and markets.

These three factors would be nothing if it were not for the glue of community and authenticity that causes them to combine to create the true St. Ives spirit. The arts, for example, would be just a tourist attraction were it not for the presence of scores of working artists and craftspeople in the town. It is

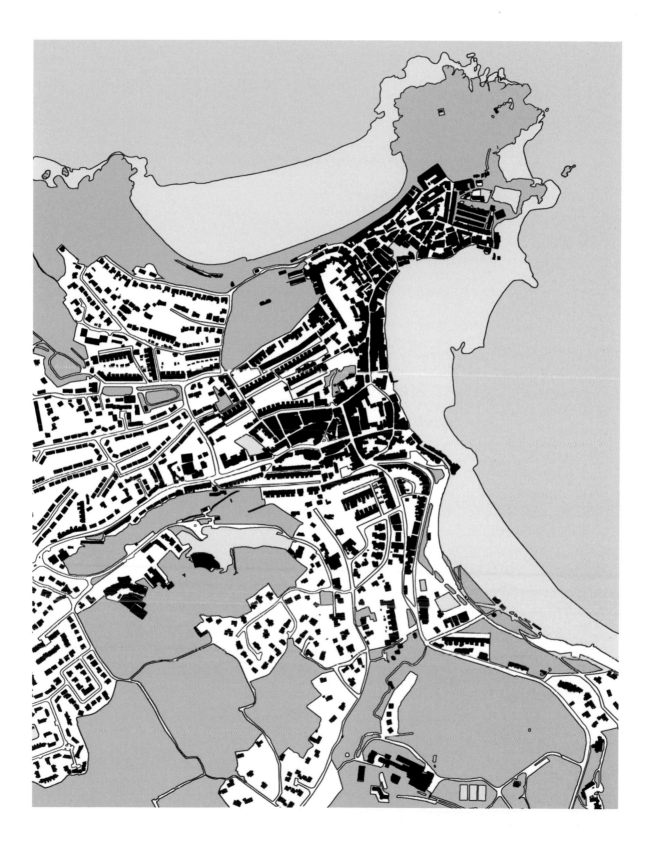

SIR JOHN BETJEMANIC FOR ST IVES

The best place to take in the air is St. Ives!
Where artistic people lead artistic lives!
Buzzing like artistic bees buzz in hives!

The sea is the backdrop, the sea and the sky!
As the streets seem to shimmer, the clouds seem to fly!
In a good way, this place is like watching paint dry!

But the paint never dries on this jewel of a town
As the leaves turn from green to that rare Cornish brown
Reinvention's the name in these streets of reknown!

For a place like St. Ives simply cannot sit still!
It's a triumph of energy, triumph of will!
It's a gorgeous pot plant on the World's window-sill!

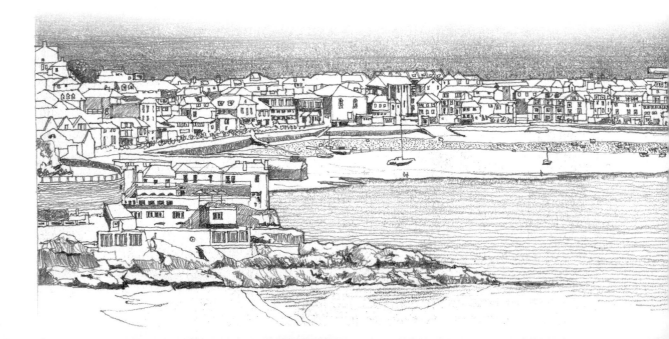

The St. Ives galleries are so attractive because the art is made by real artists and not for tourists.

Barbara Hepworth's garden, now open as a visitor attraction

the fact that so much of St. Ives' artistic work is not done for the tourist that makes it so attractive. Another example of this authenticity is the fishing industry, which has been revived at a time when other fishing ports have declined. The authenticity of St. Ives is also about its sense of community. It is the same size as Ludlow and there is a similar sense that all of the key people know each other, serve together on the Town Council and take a real pride and ownership in the town.

These elements combine in St. Ives to create a unique place. The quality of its environment, its fine shops and restaurants, its sense of community, its traditional fishing industry, its beaches and indeed its light and colour, make it more like St. Jean de Luz in south-west France or Cadaques on the Costa Brava. In this respect, St. Ives might be said to be leading a revival of the British seaside resort, creating a quality image that attracts visitors and residents throughout the year.

Left: The Tate in St. Ives is one of only three-all-year round tourist attractions in Cornwall.

Below Left: One of Ludlow's renovated buildings, with a carving of the building, the architect and client – a statement of commitment not found in modern contracting.

Threads and Themes

The three towns are very different but they have all, in their own way, solved the same set of problems – how to respond to a changing world where you can no longer rely on the loyalty of your catchment population or the stability of local employers. They have all asked the question – what is the role of this town and how must it evolve in the future? Despite their differences, some of the answers are remarkably similar.

Outsiders are attracted and made welcome. Visitors, new residents or students increase the spending power of a town and its well of talent and enthusiasm. As with the art of seduction, these outsiders will not be attracted by a head-on attack but by the feigned indifference of a genuine and authentic place. The five key ingredients are:

☐ Making people feel at home: If attracting incomers is like seduction, keeping them is like a good marriage. What the three towns have in common is a strong community that embraces the stranger, reflecting an inner self-confidence that doesn't feel threatened by outsiders.

☐ Paying attention to quality of life: A place that is good to live in is also a good place to visit. All three towns have concentrated on the quality of life of the existing community – improving the town for the benefit of the people who live there, not for the sake of visitors.

☐ Recognising the value of good food: All three towns have focused on food by promoting quality local produce to support local businesses, fishermen and farmers, creating jobs for local people and enhancing the experience for locals and visitors.

☐ The importance of arts and culture: From Lincoln's investment in cultural institutions to Ludlow's community-run arts centre and festivals, to the artists and galleries of St. Ives, these three

Beach at St. Ives. Below: Local fresh fish shop.

towns have used the arts as a way to project a quality, upmarket image.

☐ Taking care of the environment: Of course it helps to be beautiful. Good-quality conservation work is important, but this does not mean that new buildings cannot be contemporary, such as Ludlow's new library, the Tate in St. Ives or The Collection in Lincoln.

However, the real beauty of a place lies in the ever-changing vitality of its streets, shops and activities, the way that its people are engaged and involved in the life of the town, and how it meets their everyday needs and enhances their lives. This is partly a result of its design but is also about the way a town is organised, the way uses are allowed to mix and the way that density of people and activity is encouraged. This is urbanism, and it can be equally alive in a good town as it is in a great city.

Reference
1 Lynas, Mark, *New Statesman*, 25 September 2006.

Brian Evans

Neighbourhoods:
The basic building blocks of the city

The purpose of this piece is not to define the neighbourhood, or to lock down a definition that's good for all time; rather it is to begin a journey towards understanding the neighbourhoods of the British Isles and in particular to diagnose what the Academy has learned from studying three neighbourhoods – the Merchant City in Glasgow, Clifton in Bristol and Clerkenwell in London. But we need to start somewhere, and have some reference for the journey, even if, as Oscar Wilde's stranger would have it, we 'wouldn't start from here'.

In his discourse on districts, Kevin Lynch finds the essential nature of neighbourhood being formed partly of character, and by extension culture, and partly of function. He never quite resolves this dichotomy. For Lynch, districts are:

> the relatively large city areas which the observer can mentally go inside of, and which have some common character. They can be recognised internally, and occasionally can be used as external reference as a person goes by or toward them. … even where they were not used for orientation, districts were still an important and satisfying part of the experience of living in the city.[1]

This is Lynch writing in his seminal The Image of the City, originally published in 1960. He determines districts by physical characteristics that are primarily thematic and based on a variety of components: texture, space, form, detail, symbol, building type, use, activity, inhabitants, degree of maintenance and topography.

By the 1980s (with his earlier book still going strong), Lynch published Good City Form and begins to get down to the concept of neighbourhood itself.

Merchant City signing.

Ingram Square (Left) and the Italian Centre (Right)
in the Merchant City.

The idea of the urban neighborhood has ridden a professional rollercoaster. In the first quarter of this century, it was a unit of social analysis used by pioneers in urban sociology. The idea then grew that the neighborhood was the proper territorial base of a socially supportive group, among whom there would be many personal contacts. Planning theorists, reassured by their organic models, picked up the idea of the neighborhood as the basic building block of a city. It was to be a defined spatial unit, free of through traffic and as self-sufficient in daily services as possible. The unit was sized to the catchment area of the typical elementary school, and the catchments of other services were to be adjusted to this module, or to integral multiples of it. This idea is still influential in city design throughout the world. It has the advantages of simplicity for design; it provides quiet streets; it insures some fit of services to demand.[2]

The concept of a neighbourhood as an area large enough to require a primary school was part of Clarence Perry's definition published as part of the First Regional Plan for New York[3]. Later, the idea fell from favour because it did not correspond to conditions in (primarily North American) cities where contacts were based on work, family or leisure pursuits rather than place; as a result, using the concept of neighbourhood in planning caused a mismatch with the provision of services.

But while the neighbourhood was thoroughly debunked by modernist planning theory and practice, the threats from urban renewal – expressways, housing renewal, expansion of institutions – caused a backlash of resistance at community and local level. This demonstrated that, even when work and family relationships were dispersed far beyond the neighbourhood, there was still no better unit of social organisation to address the bigger and frequently threatening issues of urban life. Issue-orientated and change-resistant rather than change-generating, the local neighbourhood is frequently important to the way people conceive of a city in their minds. It may not be central to social or even business relationships, but it is, together with primary routes, key to the legibility of the city, an

Fruitmarket performance venue in Glasgow.

essential part of what Lynch describes as people's 'mental equipment'.

The doyenne of the neighbourhood was, of course, Jane Jacobs, the 'Grande Dame' of planning – after all these decades her views remain as fresh, direct and relevant as when she first laid them down:

> A successful city neighbourhood is a place that keeps sufficiently abreast of its problems so it is not destroyed by them. An unsuccessful neighbourhood is a place that is overwhelmed by its defects ... and is progressively more helpless before them.[4]

This quote provides a succinct point of departure for considering three particular neighbourhoods and for examining their similarities, differences and distinctive qualities.

The Merchant City in Glasgow is a unique place laid out to an historic offset grid with vistas closed by the mansion houses of tobacco merchants from whom the neighbourhood takes its name. In the decades that followed, its character changed to warehouses and wholesale markets, all of which have left a legacy of fine and varied building stock. In the last 25 years or so, a series of projects – Ingram Square, the Italian Centre, Cochrane Square and the conversion and refurbishment of the former Fruitmarket – have helped to set new standards for development in inner city neighbourhoods in Britain. The Merchant City Festival now has over 600 artists providing entertainment in a wide range of activities from the visual arts and comedy to cooking and fashion.

This is the Greenwich Village of Glasgow – an urban village with a metropolitan character – a mix of national (Scottish Youth Theatre), city (the City Halls, the Tron Theatre, the Gallery of Modern Art (GoMA)) and local clubs, cafés and bars; as Richard Florida would put it, the Merchant City is 'BoHo' Glasgow[5].

Figure ground Merchant City Glasgow

MERCHANT CITY, GLASGOW

Looked at on a map this is a tight net of streets
But it's more than that. Much more.
It's the sound of laughter, and the age old sound
Of music leaking through an open door
And the music is the music of renewal;
A tune that sounds different every single day
As the lessons of history from that hard, hard school
Are learned; not forgotten, not tidied away.
Looked at on the map this is angles and lines
But the reality's shifting, the reality moves
From a warehousescape where the moonlight shines
And lights up a vista that needs a good scrub
To a web of renewal, an idea made real,
A vast global menu, a cultural hub.

Lunching al fresco and careful infill development in the Merchant City.

The area has a reputation as a centre for cutting-edge bars, restaurants and hotels as well as small creative businesses, independent retailers, artists' workshops and galleries. It is home to the best part of 1,000 businesses; indeed, nearly 50 new enterprises moved into the area in 2005/06. Almost three-quarters of the street frontages have active ground-floor uses – shops, cafés, bars and restaurants.

Clifton in Bristol is quite different. It enjoys a dramatic topography that was exploited through the creation of major crescents and terraces which follow the contours and look down to the harbour. The Victorian expansions extend up to the edge of the Downs, taking advantage of their elevated position overlooking the city. Clifton benefits from Georgian and early Victorian terraced houses that have proved to be very adaptable – 'robust' in urban design-speak – for small purpose-built shops in the centre. Mews buildings have also been adapted to modern needs, and outdated service uses and commercial buildings have been converted successfully to provide new housing. A former furniture repository has more recently become a successful shopping arcade.

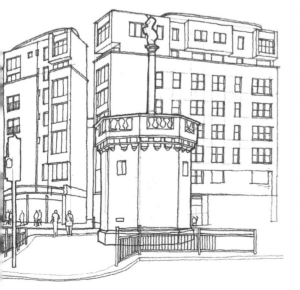

The third of the neighbourhoods, Clerkenwell in London, has a strong sense of place that is reinforced by the activities of local interest groups and now by local authority policy. Clerkenwell today builds on its significant heritage, and contemporary development, including some public realm improvements, is influenced by this context and has proved particularly attractive to design professionals (e.g. Clerkenwell Workshop). The area has several sub-areas, from the predominantly business zones

Homes for the Future from Glasgow City of Architecture & Design 1999.

to the quieter residential enclaves to the north. Both display distinctive qualities and contribute to the overall character of the area, with Exmouth Market as its fulcrum. Together with Clerkenwell Green, it provides a focus for social interaction. Clerkenwell has a clear and interconnected street network and is well integrated into London's transport system with ready access to buses and tube along all surrounding streets. Within the neighbourhood, the area is very accessible on foot, but the lack of traffic management by the local authority means that traffic often moves at a speed that is greater than desirable within a walkable, liveable neighbourhood.

The characteristics of the three neighbourhoods are quite different and mirror the way they are used, managed and maintained. There is a clear vision and strategy for the future of the Merchant City that involves all key partners – public sector, business and the community – and a dedicated initiative for management of the area with an on-site project office. The aim of the Merchant City Initiative is to revitalise social and economic conditions and deliver a public realm of European quality to support

this endeavour. The area benefits from strong local management arrangements led by the Merchant City Traders Association. In turn, this has engendered strong private sector commitment built on public sector support and community confidence.

Clifton is well managed, inclusive, fair and well run. There is a reliance on the energies of volunteer groups (Bristol Civic Society, Clifton and Hotwells Improvement Society, Bristol Visual and Environmental Group) and evidence of people working together to a collective vision for the area from as early as the 1970s with the initial Conservation Area designation. A policy of careful repair and renewal has been pursued through projects involving the community and the City Council that has enabled the regeneration of set-piece architectural groups (e.g. Royal York Crescent, Paragon and successful conservation of the whole area). The neighbourhood is well maintained, with an emphasis on public spaces and green areas.

By contrast, the clearest expression of a collective vision for Clerkenwell can be found in the UDP

Glasgow Green, the city's oldest park.

Candleriggs and the public realm.

(Unitary Development Plan) and, while that finely tuned and official instrument of action seeks to 'preserve and enhance the special character of the area', there is no dedicated body or agency for Clerkenwell with any special responsibilities. To be fair, the local authority aims to achieve this UDP objective by relying on the interests and application of others (e.g. Clerkenwell Green Association's aim to promote fine craft and design skills in the area). There is some evidence that enhancements to the public realm involve inclusive processes; for example, proposals are explained and comments invited through information boards on site although such techniques would now be seen as simply 'first base' in most dynamic urban areas in Britain and Ireland.

What of the communities that inhabit these places? Their health and diversity are surely some of the most significant indices in urban diagnostics.

The Merchant City community benefits from people of all ages – people come to live, to work, to visit and to pass time. There is a mixed permanent

community of young people, students, professional couples, families and elderly people. It is very much a metropolitan community, with a core stable base and a fluid, transient component.

In Clifton, there is a strong local pride reflecting a deep community spirit. Nonetheless, there is a significant incoming population of young, upwardly mobile people and a new student population each year. The strong tradition of local activism helps protect its historic distinctiveness from development, and ensures that the local character is retained. The historic context is carefully considered in all new development, by discussion and debate between the local amenity societies and the planning authority. Nevertheless, much new development in the area employs good contemporary design.

Both Clifton and the Merchant City are highly valued as places to live, to work and to relax; for many, these are premier neighbourhood locations in Bristol and Glasgow respectively. The balance in each is slightly different. The Merchant City leads with its metropolitan character within which a local commu-

Left: Figure ground of Clifton, Below: Clifton Gorge and the Clifton Suspension Bridge.

nity is built and nurtured. Clifton, on the other hand, has a more pronounced community and a local focus with a wide age range from students to elderly residents. Clifton attracts many visitors, enjoying its village atmosphere, the shops, leisure facilities and fine open spaces. It is a much visited tourist attraction for Bristol, bringing visitors from abroad to see the architecture, the suspension bridge, the gorge and the zoo.

These attributes are also strong in Clerkenwell. There is much evidence that the culture of local people (residents and businesses) is expressed in physical and social structures: a wide range of residential accommodation exists in the area (flats/houses) with a varied mix of tenures. One local businessman applauded the 'stock of misfit buildings' as essential to the life and character of the area. Socially, many interest groups exist (Business Junction, Clerkenwell Green Association, etc.) and events are held regularly such as the Clerkenwell

Biennale. Public art is in evidence, including temporary installations such as 'Oxygen' at Clerkenwell Green. With its wide range of housing type and tenure, Clerkenwell attracts people of all ages for living and for work. The area is highly accessible (within the sector bounded by Farringdon Road, Crosswell Road, Cowcross Street and Pentonville Road) and some parts of the neighbourhood are particularly vibrant with active frontages, notably Cowcross Street, Clerkenwell Green and Exmouth Market.

The combination of community characteristics and management arrangements is likely to be key in contributing to that elusive quality of urbanism – activity – the vitality of a place, its ambience, its 'street-cred'.

The Merchant City exhibits all of the qualities of traditional urbanism – passive supervision from apartment windows and shopfronts as well as outdoor eating and drinking across long periods

CLIFTON SUSPENDED

Hold your arms wide apart, like this,
Like a fisherman praising a fish
To describe that incredible bridge.

Then bring your hands together this way
To applaud Clifton's buildings, each day
Renewed by light and cloud interplay.

Then stand on a corner and think
Of this 'place on a hill', this link
With the past and the future; drink

In the views that astonish the brain;
Then turn round a corner and drink them again!

Bottom Left: The Lanes of Clifton, Below: Clifton's terraces are its most famous attribute while its gardens are ideal greenspaces for community living (bottom).

Adaptive reuse in Cowcross Street.

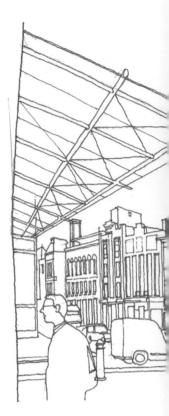

of the day, beginning around 8 a.m. and extending well into the evening and early morning hours. Although this is an inner urban neighbourhood, the River Clyde linear park is within a five-minute walk, as is Glasgow Green – the city's oldest public park – which extends to some 80 hectares.

Largely as a result of continued support and investment led by public agencies, there has been a considerable rise in property values since the early 1990s and this in turn has helped to fuel a renewed level of economic activity. Strathclyde University campus lies adjacent to the Merchant City and, in a joint venture with Scottish Enterprise, the City Council and the private sector, the university has driven forward the development of a £60 million 'Science City', which includes new private, social and student housing. The new buildings respect the original street pattern, creating improved streets and squares as the development continues with active ground-floor frontages including shops, cafés, restaurants and bars. In addition to a series

of 'exemplar' projects to improve the public realm (including the award-winning Royal Exchange Square, Buchanan Street and Argyll Street), over £2.5 million is spent annually improving the quality of streets and footpaths throughout the Merchant City, rolling out a programme based on the seminal public realm strategy for the city centre produced in the 1990s.

The whole intent behind the Merchant City Initiative is to make the neighbourhood one of the principal areas that help to sustain the City of Glasgow itself by providing a wide and attractive range of places to live, to work and to visit. The population of the area is now over 3,000, with two active community councils. Most of its residents walk to work, while management of the neighbourhood encourages pedestrian and public transport over the car.

In Clifton, the public realm is managed by Bristol City Council and local garden committees. Management groups have responded sensitively over time

CLERKENWELL

Come here to eat, come here to drink,
As the sun sets on the city then come down here to think
About what Clerkenwell is, and how we can define it
How we can undilute it, and preserve it, and refine it
And help it to develop and never to stand still;
And sing a hymn of praise to Clerkenwell!

Come here to see, come here to be seen
As the day gets filled to bursting and the hours in between
Glow with what this marvellous district has to offer
It's a star in evening skies, or a gold coin in a coffer.
There's nowhere you can get a smarter, cooler urban thrill
Than the shining destination that we call Clerkenwell!

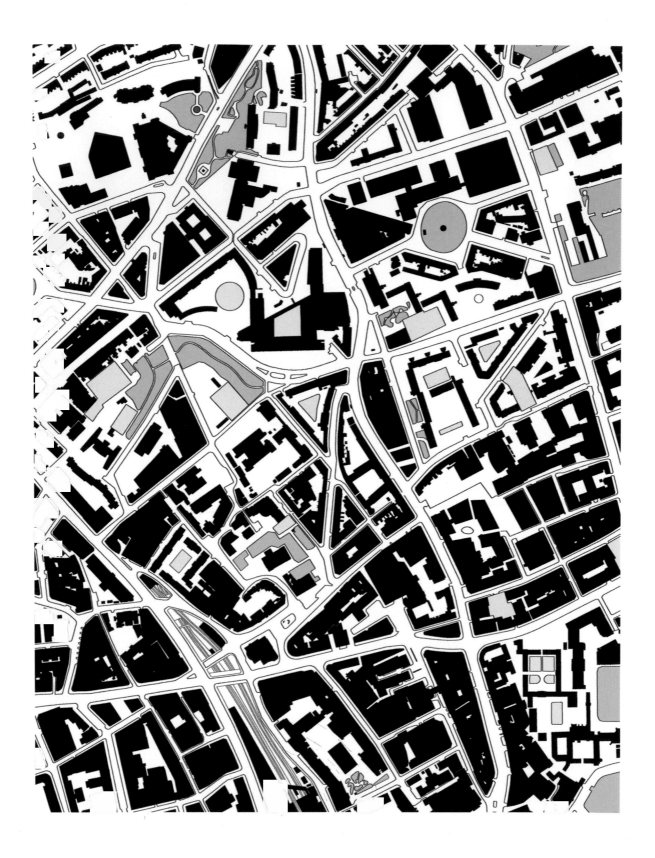

Public realm improvements in Clerkenwell.

to changes in patterns of use, recreational trends, demand for events, entertainments and increased use by the public. The shopping heart of the area is a compact network of charming streets, with continuous active frontages set in a range of historic styles and periods. Cafés, restaurants and bars provide pleasant contrast to the retail environment, generating activity from the first café opening in the morning to the last bar closing at night. Most of the upper floors are in residential use, many with separate access. A particular strength of the shopping offer is the high level of independent traders and there are indications of some adjustment by chain store multiples (e.g. Tesco Metro). Active and passive surveillance of the urban environment is high. To an extent, Clifton has been almost too successful in drawing visitors and creating a destination for

evening leisure activity. Residents report the usual frustrations and concerns about drink-related noise and disturbance late in the evening, but overall this is viewed as minor when compared with other parts of Bristol or other cities.

Clifton is very well provided with well-maintained historic parks and gardens. Immediately adjacent to the area are the Downs and just across the suspension bridge through Leigh Woods is the Ashton Court country park with open countryside beyond. The area has a high level of car ownership, but there is limited parking on-street and very little opportunity to increase it off-street. There are good public transport links with the city centre, including a local train service that links through to the main railway station at Temple Meads. The intimate and

The organic and cohesive townscape of Clerkenwell has been retained.

dense street pattern is complemented by a network of footpaths that make walking an attractive alternative to the car. Many walk to work in the city centre some 20 minutes away.

In Clerkenwell, the urban environment for the most part supports natural surveillance. This is limited in certain areas by constraints posed by historic buildings – part of the character of the area, although some are of a 'warehouse' nature with limited public frontages and a more forbidding character in the hours of darkness. However, this is counterbalanced by the civic pride and investment in the area that encourages civilised and responsible behaviour. Located on the edge of the City of London, Clerkenwell has limited public parks, but a wide range of parks and spaces lie within easy walking distance, including the Inns of Court. Clerkenwell Green has recently been refurbished and lies to the south of Exmouth Market. The area has a substantial number of mature trees, especially in gardens and churchyards.

Commercial activity is successfully encouraged and there are several examples of recently completed projects (e.g. Clerkenwell Workshop). There is no evidence of a proactive programme to create employment. Rather, planning policy seeks to foster a range of employment opportunities. People from local businesses suggest that the economic success of the area has occurred in spite of local authority policies from the late 1970s through to the 1990s. But the success is now fostered and embraced in policy. The growth of the design industries is promoted actively by non-governmental agencies such as the Clerkenwell Green Association.

Local businesses cite planning policies aimed at protecting the character of Clerkenwell as reasons for investing in the area. The image and quality of space is seen as particularly important to the creative industries. This sense of identity is also important to the services – restaurants etc. – that seek to

New infill development with in-town supermarket in Clerkenwell. Below: New office developments complement the historic townscape.

provide an image appropriate to their clientele. It proved more difficult to investigate environmental and social sustainability in Clerkenwell. There is, however, evidence of an active 'cultural' life that makes use of public space and displays pride in the character and history of the place.

In urbanism, there is no substitute for getting out and walking about – looking, talking, partaking of city life. It was ever thus and it's the only way to find out for sure what the dynamic of a place really is. The three neighbourhoods considered here are different in terms of their geography, demographics and role in their cities, but they are all broadly of a similar size – Lynch's 'basic building block of the city'. Significantly, they all pass Jane Jacobs' critical test – of confronting and resolving their problems, albeit in quite different ways. Vive la difference!

References
1   Lynch, Kevin, *The Image of the City*, MIT Press, 1960.
2   Lynch, Kevin, *Good City Form*, MIT Press, 1981.
3   Barnett, Jonathan, *The Elusive City: Five Centuries of Design, Ambition and Miscalculation*, Harper & Row, 1986.
4   Jacobs, Jane, *The Death and Life of Great American Cities*, Jonathan Cape, 1962.
5   Florida, Richard, *The Rise of the Creative Class*, Basic Books, 2002.

David Taylor

Great Streets

Brick Lane, Marylebone High Street & The Royal Mile

What makes a great street? Some might talk of beauty, harmony, form and function, but the life of a place is a product of the people who use it – from individuals shopping for their daily needs to whole cultures demonstrating their values through the collective use of a space.

Cities are built over time by people. As we focus in from an aerial overview, coming right down to street level, to the human scale, we realise that the life of the city derives from the way that places are used by people going about their daily routine. Sometimes places provide the stage for historically significant events – on these occasions the place can take on a heightened importance for peoples and for cultures.

The Royal Mile in Edinburgh is defined by its unique topography and townscape setting, and reveals numerous stories of Scotland's history and life. Brick Lane's location on the edge of the City of London gives an insight into the challenges of incomers settling in and enriching their communities. Marylebone High Street, once on the city's edge, is now a place which has maintained a local and neighbourly feel after being subsumed into the fabric of a great city.

Descriptions of these particular streets reflect people's appreciation of them based on their personal experiences. Comparing and contrasting them provides an opportunity to identify common themes that influence the way they work. More importantly, their distinct characteristics help to inform us about how the qualities of a place evolve and to identify the factors that can influence their design.

Each of the three streets tells a different story. Each has been shaped by its unique geographical circumstances and the way it has been used. Each now enjoys a wider reputation that draws people to it. They host different architectural styles and have different relationships to their surrounding neighbourhood. Their movement patterns vary but all have been changed in the 20th century in ways that have diminished them. Today, we can imagine how their future development will face new challenges, new opportunities and new chapters in the stories of the streets themselves and of our changing relationship with the urban environment.

Streets inserted off the Royal Mile attempted to open it to through traffic.

Left: Brick Lane. The historic street is embedded in an eclectic jumble of urban forms.

Middle: Marylebone High Street. The crooked shape of the historic field boundary can clearly be seen in the grid of Georgian development.

Right: The Royal Mile is defined by its geography, steeply dropping down into valleys north and south, and a sheer cliff to the west.

Figure ground: the Royal Mile.

Left: The Royal Mile contains the major institutions of Scotland, and is an important public space that hosts many events.
Middle: Ancient and modern come together in new public spaces. Right: The traditional buildings show alteration over the years.

The Royal Mile – a street of history

The City's and at times the Nation's front room, a mercat, or place or elongated square; the container for every-day upheaval and intellectual ferment; a history of Scottish architecture written in wood and stone; and a history of Scottish thought. Geddes lived and worked here, and there can be no better demonstration of this.[1]

As the historical spine of Scotland's capital city, the Royal Mile serves as an example of how a street can tell the story of a nation. But it can also help to tell the story of how and why people build cities. Since ancient times, Edinburgh was a settlement that benefited from the defensive properties of the landscape and ease of access to the sea. The Royal Mile starts at Castle Rock, a uniquely command-ing natural bastion that is sheer on three sides. This stunning geological feature and the mighty citadel of Edinburgh Castle tower over the New Town below. The Castle caps a street that does not sit in the urban fabric. It is the urban fabric. Architecture and topography blend seamlessly, in a way that no other street in Britain does so well.

As history moves from medieval to modern, so the Royal Mile slopes downwards from the fourth side of the Castle. The front door of the Castle opens onto an historic broad esplanade – a parade ground, a space of public assembly and home to the annual military tattoo and the annual Hogmanay celebra-tions. As the Royal Mile's name changes from the Esplanade to Castlehill, from Lawnmarket to High Street to Canongate, various buildings command attention and record many significant events. Each in turn is central to the public and cultural life of Scot-land – St. Giles' Cathedral and the Assembly Hall of the Church of Scotland, the High Court of Justiciary and Old Parliament House, where the Scottish Parlia-ment was dissolved after the signing of the Act of Union in 1707. Other institutions such as the head-quarters of the Bank of Scotland and The Scotsman newspaper lie but a block from the Royal Mile.

In its central section, the Royal Mile more resembles a familiar city street, with parallel walls of shops and apartments above. The City Wall was located near

THE ROYAL MILE

The wind fresh, the air clear
The air clear, the wind fresh
You feel like royalty walking up here:
At Festival time in a leafleted rush
Or on a silent afternoon
With the castle like a promise
And the Camera Obscura
Holding streetlife up to share,
And the Parliament's
modern majesty

Like a new vessel on an old shore.
This feels more like a lifetime than a mile
In the best way, of course;
The stone old, the sky true,
Each walk up here sees the mile renewed.
The wind fresh, the air clear
The air clear, the wind fresh
The stone old, the sky true
Each walk up here sees
the mile renewed ...

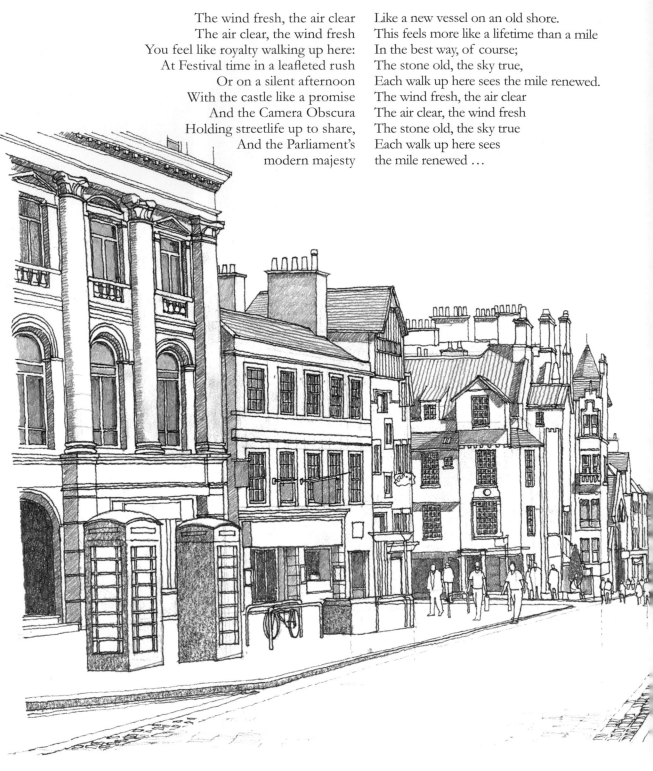

the head of Canongate, where you can find The World's End, one of Edinburgh's 'bars with character'. In 1856, when the city was greatly expanded, the Royal Mile was formally extended along its final, narrowest stretch to the Palace of Holyroodhouse, the Queen's official residence in Scotland. The Victorian restructuring of the city, to connect the New Town to the Royal Mile, saw the introduction of streets winding up from the valley below of a scale that does not detract from the historic quality of the place. They feel right, and approaching from these surrounding streets the three-dimensional form and scale of the Royal Mile are suddenly revealed.

Whereas once the country defended its interests from the high ground of the Castle, today it proclaims them from the basin of the new Scottish Parliament. The Parliament presents an iconic architecture of allegory and myth – of a dialogue with the land not the city. Facing away from the Royal Mile, it has turned its back on the historic context of the street and fragments the block structure of the Old Town. But from within, the debating chamber overlooks Edinburgh's heroic geology beneath the extinct volcano of Arthur's Seat.

The Royal Mile was one of the places where the foundations of the Enlightenment and Empire were laid. Today, it plays host to millions of visitors who drive the booming tourist economy. Where the Castle Esplanade first offered a parade ground for military might, a tradition kept alive by the annual military tattoo, the Royal Mile is also a principal venue for the street theatre of the Edinburgh Festival. This international cultural showcase now reflects Britain's global position as a service economy. The Edinburgh Festival and Hogmanay party now define the Scottish capital as an international festival city, while the Royal Mile has returned to a space defined by pedestrians and is both a dramatic location and backdrop for the city.

This traditionally working-class area stands in the shadow of London's world-leading business district.

Brick Lane – a street of opportunity

I was moved to tears to see bearded Jews and Irish Catholic dockers standing up to stop Mosley. I shall never forget that as long as I live, how working-class people could get together to oppose the evil of racism[2].

By contrast with those of the Royal Mile, Brick Lane's origins are rather modest. This street reveals a great deal about changing economic circumstances. In fact, if the Royal Mile tells the story of a nation in its landscape and culture, Brick Lane tells the story of cultures alien to the landscape and outside the nation's civic and political establishment. First named in 1550, Brick Lane was a narrow lane located less than a kilometre to the north-east of the old city walls. As the name suggests, it provided access to and from brick and tile manufacturing sites. Because this land lay outside the walls, it was not under the influence of the guilds that controlled labour within the city itself. The surrounding area has always contained a mix of residential and industrial buildings and today the architectural styles vary from terraced Georgian town houses to unimposing light industrial buildings and low-cost 1960s office blocks. The continual and adaptive reuse of

buildings is central to the character of the area and, although various buildings have been demolished over the years, Brick Lane retains the character of a narrow Georgian street, which in part benefits its nature as a pedestrian-friendly space.

Outside the official city, the neighbourhood of Brick Lane was a home to non-conformists and immigrants fleeing persecution or poor economic opportunities elsewhere. French Protestant Huguenot weavers arrived in 1685 from continental Europe. Two hundred years later, Eastern European Jews arrived, further consolidating the textile industry. From the 1940s, Muslims from Bengal started to arrive, many from the Merchant Navy. The process continued through the 1960s and by the 1970s almost 95 per cent of the local population were working in the textile industry, in conditions likened to those of a century before.

Figure ground: Brick Lane.

Post-industrial regeneration marks a transition from the past to the future.

Brick Lane typifies many areas of the inner East End where the prevailing wind always blows from west to east. When in 1660 it was chosen as the site for a major brewery, later becoming the Truman Brewery, the foul-smelling emissions drifted eastwards down the Thames Estuary and not towards the City of London immediately to the west.

Throughout the 20th century, rising affluence prompted migration to more pleasant areas north and west of central London. By the 1980s, increased competition of low-cost manufacturing from abroad created economic decline, and this led the London Borough of Tower Hamlets to begin a regeneration strategy that continues today. The cultural identity of Brick Lane was boosted as the heart of 'Bangla-town', an equivalent to the 'Chinatown brand' long familiar in many cities, includ-

ing London. The southern end of the street is now marked by an ornate Bengali gateway, the annual Baishaki Mela celebrates Bangladesh's arts, music and culture, and the street's large number of curry houses now herald their role annually via the Brick Lane International Curry Festival.

The changing nature of Brick Lane as a conduit for transient migrant communities can be seen in the way its architectural form has been adapted for different uses over different generations. The Jamme Masjid mosque, now one of the most important centres for Islamic worship in London, was built in 1744 as a church for the French Protestant community. It was later bought by Wesleyans and by 1900 had become a Jewish synagogue. The Truman Brewery, once the largest employer on the street, has been transformed into offices for innovative new

The street changes its form throughout its length but with a constant mix of residential and commercial use.

Small creative businesses such as boutique fashion, music and new media bring new economic life to the area. Cultures from around the world have settled in this area over many centuries.

BRICK BY BRICK

Look at this lane, built brick-by-brick
Into a market, a magical space, a gathering of voices
A joyful dove-from-a-top-hat trick
A celebration of difference, multiplicity of choices

And the best curry you'll ever taste!

Look at this lane, built brick-by-brick
It's an example of how a place might function;
How ideas and concepts, once thrown, might stick
And there's never just the obvious turn at the junction ...

And the best curry you'll ever taste!

So raise a glass to the place they
call Brick Lane;

Delightful in the sunshine,
exciting in the rain.

Above: Brick Lane is famous as London's centre for Bengali cuisine and has long been a centre for textile manufacture and distribution.

Right: Bars, clubs and pedestrian-friendly environment help attract a young, professional crowd.

businesses in fashion, music and the digital media, and contains nightclubs, bars, cafés and galleries.

Attracting young, creative professionals into the area has been central to its economic development, but as the office blocks of the City move ever closer, Brick Lane may soon face more severe challenges. With economic growth linked to property prices, will today's Bangladeshi community follow the pattern of their predecessors by selling up and moving on? As the eastern edge of the city changes, Brick Lane may be swallowed up by surrounding regeneration and development. New transport routes, such as the extension of the Underground to serve London's Olympics site in 2012 and the Crossrail project to link the city's railway stations will precipitate a massive change in the economic nature of the street and its surrounding area.

Figure ground: Marylebone High Street.

A traditional small-town high street has been created in the centre of London.

Marylebone High Street – a street with a vision

Marylebone is seen as something of a blueprint for how to regenerate a high street in an imaginative and appealing way which provides a strong alternative to the rather bland 'clone' offerings elsewhere[3].

The last of the three 'great streets' lies in London's West End and offers an example of how Brick Lane in the East End might manage its future. Marylebone High Street began life as a field boundary between farmland off London's north-west edge. Today, at the southern end of the street, the land dips down where the lost River Tyburn once flowed. The modern shape of Marylebone Lane immediately to the south still follows its course, and the name comes from the church of St. Mary's once located here.

Around 1400, the church was moved to a site at the top of Marylebone High Street, where its churchyard now forms a public park. The Manor of Tyburn, as is recorded in the Domesday Book, defined an estate that reached north of Oxford Street, encompassing the area now occupied by Regent's Park and London Zoo. In 1711, the estate passed to new owners who responded to the demand for high-quality housing by creating a masterplan for the area. A grid of terraced streets stretching from Cavendish Square

Quality food provision is central to the regeneration strategy.

to the east subsumed the old village high street but retained its geometry, and this explains the alignment of Marylebone High Street today.

Although now in the heart of London's West End, with its local landmarks including numerous embassies and major department stores, the estate used to be a fashionable suburb on the rural fringe. As London spread outwards, Marylebone High Street was swallowed up in the expanding city and its original function diminished. Despite its central location, good mix of tenures and excellent transport provision, economic recessions had left the street in a poor condition by the late 20th century, with many of its shops empty.

In 1994, the Howard de Walden Estate, which had owned the area since 1879, implemented a strategy to revitalise it. The vision was to renew the street as a neighbourhood centre, with the characteristics of a traditional English high street, where quality small retailers sat alongside familiar stores supplying essentials. To achieve this, the estate began buying back retail leases that had long been sold on, and inviting particular retailers and restaurants into the area. Two large retailers, Terence Conran's furniture store and the upmarket Waitrose chain, were brought in to anchor the north and south ends of the street by employing the letting principles of the shopping mall, but in the street outside.

MARYLEBONE HIGH STREET

You can see this street from high up in space,
See the coffee cups catching the light
And the spoons and the plates and the outdoor tables
Long into the Summer night.

This is High Street as bloodstream, street as connection.
Streetlife and real life and streetlife as home;
Meeting and talking and walking and shopping,
As vital as New York, as stylish as Rome.

If this street didn't exist you could dream it to life:
A street that contains all the things you could need
To live in a city in this gleaming century:
High street manifesto and new High Street creed.

Café culture and independent organic food sellers are a popular attraction.

The strategy focused the street's new identity and economy on food provision, high-quality retailers and cafés. Shopping, and in particular food shopping in the Italian or French tradition, is something inherently cultural rather than a bare necessity. The estate sponsors a farmers' market that brings independently produced food into the heart of the city. Sunday has become one of the busiest shopping days in the area, and the farmers' market provides an outlet for local, organic food from small-scale producers, a process now widely recognised to be of vital importance to an environmentally sustainable future. The encouragement of this type of food distribution pre-dates the former mayor of London, Ken Livingstone's strategy to encourage organic farmers' markets in every neighbourhood in the city. The vision applied to the management of Marylebone High Street has allowed it to resist the dominance of chain stores that has adversely affected so many high streets. Research by the New Economics Foundation dubbed such places 'clone towns', where chain stores with high-profile brands provide identical goods in mass-produced interiors. The alternative to a 'clone town' is one where a variety of goods and services are available in a neighbourhood with clear individuality and character. As a local centre, which maintains a small-town feel despite being only minutes from the hectic throng of London's West End, the rejuvenated Marylebone High Street is a great success.

Flower stall, Marylebone High Street.

A shop window in Brick Lane

Great streets in context

Streets in cities serve many purposes besides carrying vehicles, and city sidewalks – the pedestrian parts of the street – serve many purposes besides carrying pedestrians. These are bound up with circulation but are not identical with it and in their own right they are at least as basic as circulation to the proper working of cities.

What makes these three streets great is that their unique properties have resulted in quality in very different ways, and this says something about the values of culture today – an interest in history and a respect for heritage, an acceptance of difference and welcoming of incomers, and a need for vision to shape a long-term future. As streets, these places are inherently about the human scale. Their sense of place is one that is understood in terms of its relationship to other places, not least the transport patterns that affect an area. Finally, coming down to the human perspective, a street is understood in terms of its life. Who uses it, for what reasons and in what ways?

Each of these streets resonates with its individual cultural context. The Royal Mile has shops selling tartans to tourists and tickets for cultural events and a busking bagpiper in full traditional dress juxtaposed with lawyers, clerics and politicians going about the business of Scotland. Brick Lane by day sees a bustling textile trade and a multi-ethnic retail offer. By night it offers an exciting and diverse range of restaurants, bars and cafés. In the regenerated centre, young creative industries buzz around the site of the Truman Brewery, and the yet-to-be regenerated north reminds us what the area was once like and how it too will inevitably be transformed. Marylebone High Street shows how economic regeneration can be successfully managed. The vision that drove the transformation of a rundown area now extends into the future, with a vision of environmentally sustainable urban living, connected to organic food production from nearby rural areas.

Looking at these streets from the human perspective, it is clear how each has survived recent and inappropriate interventions. The Victorians cut across the Royal Mile, creating new traffic routes by building ambitious bridges spanning the valley from Edinburgh New Town and installing Waverley

Performers at the Edinburgh Festival

Railway Station on the valley floor. Yet they did so on a grand scale that we value today and find hard to replicate. By contrast, the 20th-century interventions lack this 'feel' or sophistication. The requirements of horse-drawn carriages shaped the form of both Edinburgh's New Town and London's Marylebone. Their turning circles and stable mews are now forgotten influences on the urban fabric. The cars that provide accessibility to a large proportion of the population create great stress in the urban fabric and almost always at the expense of the pedestrian.

On Marylebone High Street, the Howard de Walden Estate has been able to influence the economic nature of retail and promote cultural events that help to define the neighbourhood, but traffic management remains under the control of local authority traffic engineers. Pedestrians, cyclists and cars are condensed into a space broken by mini-roundabouts and a one-way contraflow system. In places, the public realm is cluttered by pedestrian barriers and if two SUVs attempt to pass in opposite directions the street is threatened by gridlock. Yet, as London's transport strategy is subject to an increas-

ingly environmental agenda, and as long as Marylebone High Street maintains visionary leadership, its future looks optimistic.

For Brick Lane, a lack of clarity on vehicle or pedestrian priority makes it a slow-moving and not entirely relaxed street although, at its southern end, the worst impositions from the 20th century have been architectural. For the 21st century, the new developments, if well handled, promise a bright future. New rail connections will bring outside investment into an economically depressed area. To what extent its currently established population can benefit from this remains to be seen.

On the Royal Mile, the latest addition to the street is a real delight. The Scottish Storytelling Centre is an architectural asset to the street, a modern building sensitive to its surroundings that is also a cultural asset to the country. It is a venue for cultural interaction that gives new force to a great Scottish tradition, providing a platform for an old generation to educate future generations.

The design of streets, of buildings and spaces in relation to each other, says something about the land on which they are built and their relationship to other places, which over time tells the story of a culture, of a city. At the human scale, the life of a street contains countless personal stories. Together, these three great streets tell a story of British culture and the values it now holds.

References

1   Fraser, Malcolm, Architect of the Scottish Storytelling Centre
    Ref: presentation at The Academy of Urbanism.

2   Professor Bill Fishman, local resident. Ref: Day the East End
    said 'No pasaran' to Blackshirts, *The Guardian* newspaper,
    Saturday September 30, 2006
    http://www.guardian.co.uk

3   Andrew Ashenden, Chief Executive, The Howard de Walden
    Estate. Ref: Reflections on the End of an Era, *Marylebone
    Journal*, Vol 2, April 2006.
    http://www.themarylebonejournal.com

Sarah Chaplin

Places

St. Stephen's Green, Borough Market & Brindleyplace

Ray Oldenburg, in his book The Great Good Place,[1] argues that what is absent in most American cities is an informal public life, by which he means places that support the kinds of leisure activities best shared in a low-key and unstructured way. The idea of a 'third place' – a public place that is neither work nor home – Oldenburg identifies as being increasingly important, providing a necessary neutral ground in which conversation may flow, regulars may congregate and the mood can be playful. This piece considers what The Academy of Urbanism has learned from the study of three places, each of which in its own way provides exactly this kind of urban context for life to be played out: Borough Market in London, Brindleyplace in Birmingham and St. Stephen's Green in Dublin.

Although a place may be commended for sheer historic longevity, successful places are not simply a product of their ability to survive turbulent periods of urban history, to be singled out as an exemplary piece of urban form or architectural design. A place, after all, can be as transient as a fairground and as insubstantial as a picnic: both are still capable of producing a conducive atmosphere, a stimulating crowd, a good time. Thus, while Borough Market has survived for more than 250 years to emerge as London's epicurean hot spot, its success as a piece of urbanism is rooted in its capacity to engender friendly face-to-face interactions between producers and consumers, both equally passionate about quality and freshness. The canal-side location of Brindleyplace may lend it suitable historic reference points, but in truth it was a tabula rasa project which grew to be a flagship piece of urban redevelopment, resting on its future laurels more than on the past. Similarly, although St. Stephen's Green has plied customers with different wares and smart shopfronts around its urbane perimeter for the past 200 years, and its Georgian pedigree has been captured in both visual and literary form, as a place it has managed to avoid being frozen in time into a picture postcard version of itself. Its day-to-day clusterings of friends and lovers in the shade of its mature trees make it a compelling urban experience for today's busy city dweller.

Many planners would argue that the formula for a good urban place should limit its scale, its dimensions perhaps no greater than a city block, but these three places challenge this notion head-on. Brindleyplace is the product of a complex and

Below: The urbane perimeter of St. Stephen's Green.

Right: Borough Market – London's epicurean hotspot.

Bottom: Canalside Brindleyplace – emptiness activated.

The Borough Market canopy above and the classical elegance of St. Stephen's Green.

detailed masterplan, yet paradoxically as a piece of urbanism it is best appreciated at a more intimate scale: virtually no incidence of graffiti, children paddling in the pop fountain, office workers catching an art exhibition in their lunch hour. Borough Market is a large, sprawling and ill-defined semi-indoor space and thus defies spatial delineation, being more comfortable with measures that define the identity of particular hours of the day. St. Stephen's Green might seem to adhere to the classic proportions of a town square, but it too is a place that would rather not reveal its precise dimensions, and presents a host of ploys and features designed to disguise a true sense of scale.

Place as process

The secret history of places emphasises what Jonathan Raban has called the 'soft city',[2] where definitions of place are perceptual and fluid rather than objective and fixed, and neglect to account for the harder facts of governance and commercial viability. The relative paucity of research into place-making would suggest that in order to arrive at a more evidence-based understanding of urbanism, a more robust set of data is needed than what may be gleaned from randomly observed behaviours and events on a chance visit. However, when urbanism is thought of less as a product and more as a process, it is clearly revealed through these direct

MARKET PLACE, MARKET TIME

Borough Market is a place for the senses,
A crashing, dancing, shifting, moving density
Of people and foodstuffs, families and bargains,
A celebration of interaction, a huge immensity
Of sights, sounds and smells, touching and tasting
Where everything's valued and nothing is wasting
And in a world where the click of a desk-bound mouse
Is the way that we shop without leaving the house
This is shopping as theatre, shopping as life force
If shopping is racing then here comes the lead horse!
If shopping is opera then the fat lady's singing!
If shopping's celebration then get those bells ringing!
Borough Market's the place and now is a time
And if shopping's a poem then this market's the rhyme!

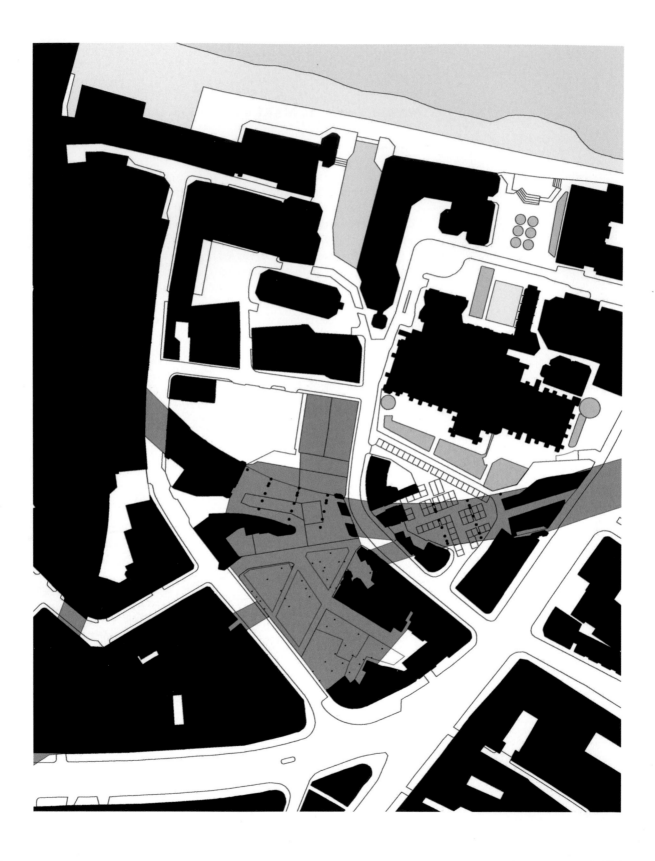

Left: Figure ground: Borough Market. Below: Aerial view, Borough Market.

encounters, which become symptomatic of its other qualities. If a place is capable of growing a sustainable community, even if only on Saturday mornings, summer evenings, or among a group of office temps, it does so in spite of the urban paradox which Raban so eloquently describes: 'To live in a city is to live in a community of people who are strangers to each other.' A successful place overcomes this, in the way that Brindleyplace, Borough Market and St. Stephen's Green all have, transforming a simple piece of real estate into somewhere people have a strong desire to be, and it is their common connection to the place that forges a sense of community.

The process of place-making does not begin with its inhabitation, however, but with the first move towards its constitution, which might involve a petition, a compulsory purchase order, or a food fair. With Brindleyplace, it began with a vision to turn a defunct post-industrial canal basin into a new mixed-use area. Successive redevelopment projects in the 1960s and 1970s had left Birmingham city centre with a poor urban environment and a negative image, and it was clear that a new strategy was needed to rescue its failing economy. The City Council conceived a sequence of 'quarters' around the city core that would be capable of breaking through the famous ring road which had come to dominate impressions of the city centre. The Convention Quarter, in which Brindleyplace falls, also contained a network of canals which it was envisaged could function as the focus of a regeneration project. Business tourism was identified as a key part of the strategic plan to revitalise Birmingham, and the International Convention Centre and its neighbouring Symphony Hall were rolled out early on, to establish a foothold for the city on the international conference circuit. However, it was not until Brindleyplace was realised that true success in this sector had been achieved.

Place-making is not only about making places but about making and growing lives and livelihoods. Place has the power to enable people to learn from each other, about each other, and about the changing world they inhabit. This is what the founder of Neal's Yard Dairy, Randolph Hodgson, thinks is so powerful about Borough Market: it is somewhere people can try, compare and learn, which in turn breeds demand for better-quality produce to be made available. Henrietta Green's first Food Lovers' Fair, which took place in 1998, kick-started the then-failing Borough Market, augmenting wholesale with retail activity, and shifting the emphasis from mass-produced to organically 'crafted' goods. The

concept of the farmers' market had already taken root in North America, but the British public were at that time less aware of issues of food quality. They were concerned, however, to preserve imposing Victorian structures, and in 1995 the trustees of Borough Market launched a design competition and commissioned architects Greig + Stephenson to refurbish the splendour of the floral hall. The Board of Trustees, however, were determined not to turn it into the next Covent Garden. Instead, what has been preserved is something of the chaotic, unassuming vitality that is characteristic of Southwark, retaining its 'under the arches' atmosphere.

More than 500 years ago, the original trustees of the market were the bridge masters, who managed lettings south of London Bridge, and used the profits to maintain it. Over time, fires, encroachment,

Night and day at Brindleyplace.

Brindleyplace is based on a series of
linked spaces

congestion and crime all created considerable challenges to
the market's survival, and eventually the City Corporation gave
up operating Borough Market, paving the way for St. Saviour's
Church to take it over and reconstitute it on a triangular piece
of land adjacent to the churchyard. By the early 19th century, it
had become a covered market squeezed between a series of
railway arches, its roof being later replaced with a lightweight
iron and glass structure that took its inspiration from the Crystal
Palace. Today's market is still run by parishioners of Southwark, and is now a registered charity.

Managerially, Brindleyplace has also had mixed fortunes and
successive changes of ownership, but over a much more
intense timescale, effectively moving from totally unviable in
1992 to totally let in 2002. Over this ten-year period, Argent,
the developers who bid for and acquired the brownfield site,
revised the masterplan to provide a more flexibly phased
development framework, and commissioned a wide range of
architects and designers to work on the different buildings. A
commitment to pursue and maintain architectural quality has
played just as much a part in this rescue operation as it has for
Borough Market, with the prestigious Ikon gallery occupying a
refurbished church and many other features preserved to help

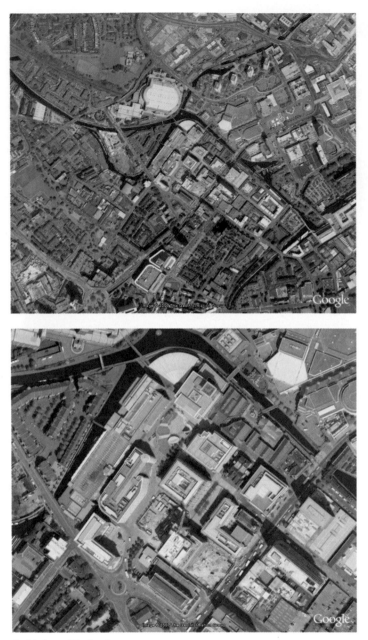

Aerial views, Brindleyplace.

create the right atmosphere. On a different scale to Borough Market, Brindleyplace nevertheless represents a similarly densely packed zone of activity, with different moods and clientele at different times of day. It caters for a more corporate client base, yet manages to avoid the overly formal urban ambience found in London Docklands and other office-orientated developments. This has a lot to do with its choice of landscaping and deliberately active edges at ground level. Though not operating as a registered charity, Argent has continued to manage the project, and supports the ripple effect of its regeneration to encompass the wider area. Brindleyplace has been instrumental in launching Broad Street as a Business Improvement District, and in raising the levels of employment in this eastern section of the city centre, creating further development impetus.

St. Stephen's Green has changed hands several times over the course of its chequered history. Once a marshy common used for grazing, the central area was enclosed by Dublin Corporation in 1664 when plots around its perimeter were sold for building. In 1814, it passed into the hands of commissioners representing the local property owners. They redesigned the park, replaced the surrounding walls with iron railings and restricted access to residents only. It was not until 1877 that an Act of Parliament was passed to reopen the Green to the public, a decision prompted by Lord Ardilaun, great-grandson of Arthur Guinness, the founder of Dublin's famous brewery. A noted philanthropist, he bought the 9-hectare park and paid for it to be landscaped as an amenity for the city. Since then, it has been in the care of the Office of Public Works, which lays on an extensive programme of events there throughout the summer.

Figure ground: Brindleyplace.

A BRINDLEYPLACE YEAR

Winter Brindley; canal shines in the low sun
And reflects the crowds shopping for Christmas,
And sitting at tables eating something lovely
And drinking in change and the way places prosper.

Spring Brindley: new ideas in new offices
Ready to grow as the year turns and grows;
From this old city now comes the new thinking,
New changing, new landscapes, new ways to work.

Summer Brindley: now this is the time
For an idea like Brindley to prosper and thrive
For the streetlife, the fountainscapes, the people
Who walk here and work here and make it alive!

Autumn Brindley: on a delicious September afternoon
You watch children by the fountain and think of the future
And the lights go on in an office at twilight
And yes. Brindleyplace is shining and smiling.

Place as experience

The defining qualities of Borough Market have to do with its continuity over space and time, gathering in people and their produce from an agricultural hinterland in much the same way that markets have always functioned. The difference here is that there is an emotional commitment to the buying and selling that goes on, something more than people making a living or shopping for the week's food. There are now self-conscious pleasures involved, which are about lingering over a richly visceral and adjectival contact with meat and poultry, cheese and wine, fruit and vegetables, something that years of cellophane wrapping and sell-by dates have denied the average city dweller.

It is all too easy to wax lyrical about the idea of a modern agora, where traders and customers know each other and there is banter as well as barter going on, but at Borough Market it exists, personalities flourish, and customs are formed. There are few contemporary urban experiences that promise something verging on the medieval, where the passage of a day's trading is palpable in the gutters, the bin stores and the back alleys. Is it authentic? Writing 'In Search of the New Public Domain', Maarten Hajer and Arnold Reijndorp argue that 'when places become too slick, when they focus too much on the supposed desires of the consumer, they become predictable and their attraction to the critical consumer as an experience diminishes'.[3]

Borough Market is without doubt a managed environment; it is pitched to a certain clientele, and attempts to divide trading hours into times when there is leisure shopping, and times when people are 'merely' trading. But it also constitutes the promise of something more real than the genetically modified and flavour-enhanced offerings we have all become accustomed to in the past few decades. Potatoes are sold still

Foodies enjoying Borough Market.

caked in soil, carrots are pleasingly misshapen, the cider is suitably cloudy, the cheeses suitably mouldy, and long-forgotten species of animal and vegetable are seemingly reintroduced. Is this what a real place has to offer? We might also ask, does the roof leak enough? Is parking problematic? Are there rats lurking in the vicinity? Do people jostle and shove and fail to observe traditional British protocols of queuing?

There is something liberating in all of this for middle-class Londoners who are desperately short

Markets are the place of social as well as financial transaction.

of quality time, and who find in Borough Market a quality experience. The by-product is that the media then begin to promote images of it synonymous with 'lifestyle', and though the presence of lifestyle is certainly not a prerequisite of good urbanism, it is a powerful indicator that a place has risen above the everyday, and merits attention as somewhere aspirational. There are many other markets in our towns and cities selling a more prosaic experience, whose typical range of goods are of variable quality. Significantly, it is not these environments that are co-opted under the banner of lifestyle, although they are a powerful part of the social and economic sustainability of a place. Borough Market simply commits to something a little more, in that profit is not the sole motivator for its market traders, and getting a bargain is not uppermost in its customers' minds.

Place as project

The naming of Brindleyplace should be seen as a critical manoeuvre: it collapses environmental connotation and denotation into a single word. As a strategy it conveys the sense that by intentionally surpassing the notion of 'Brindley Place' a deeper chord is struck, whereby identity is assured and the gap between a place name and its typological determinants is closed. Brindleyplace thereby emerges as a figure of urbanism all of its own, an urban alloy, composed of elements that cannot be disengaged. What this means on the ground is a tight-knit sequence of urban spaces that interlock around a robust and articulated constellation of buildings, where their interrelationships respond to the naming strategy by establishing a complete piece of urban fabric without qualitative gaps. In the late 19th century, this approach would have been termed a Gesamtwerk, a total project, an all-encompassing and integrated work of art, where each and every component was designed, and where the whole was greater than the sum of the parts.

With Brindleyplace the issue of aesthetic integrity associated with the Gesamtwerk is augmented by its integrity in other spheres, notably that of sustainability. Socially, there is an attempt to create a

Diversity of produce is a speciality of Borough Market.

place where the whole working day is provided for, where the notions of mixed use and the 24-hour city are fully explored. Residential accommodation comes in a variety of formats, not simply a mix of tenures or different sized units, but everything from hotel accommodation and aparthotels to rented apartments and owner-occupied homes. Birmingham City Council lays claim to a strategy of 'business tourism', in which Brindleyplace figures as a key determinant in its success, turning an industrial landscape into a place where the business community can congregate both during and after office hours.

Brindleyplace is now a fully fledged 7-hectare 'city in microcosm', merging a broad palette of urban functions and stimulating further development beyond its borders. There are moments when its architecture is showcased, and other parts of the development where the buildings or facades are appropriately low-key. It is not, therefore, an exercise in idealised or hyperbolic urban form, such as that found in places like the Disney Corporation's

The pavilion in Brindleyplace.

Celebration in Florida, but something that strives to be simultaneously dignified and down-to-earth. This is also evident in the management style, which is not founded on the rigid adherence to design codes and the self-conscious staging of events as in the case of Celebration, but a more relaxed sense of trust. This affords a genuine sense of shared ownership, and shared enjoyment of the place, the prerequisites of a lasting community.

Place as social history

As one of the three ancient commons on the periphery of medieval Dublin, St. Stephen's Green is a good example of place as social history. When the commoners' grazing land was enclosed to produce income, its edges were developed and sold off, in such a way that the green moved from being a place outside the confines of the city to become a manicured formal garden within it. This process of interiorisation is not simply about erecting railings, but is also cultural: the green has been the site of political uprisings and road blocks (notably during the Easter Rising of 1916) which have drawn it into the collective unconscious, rendering it contested space. There are, therefore,

Top: Summer tranquillity, St. Stephen's Green.
Above: Aerial view, St. Stephen's Green.

Figure ground: St. Stephen´s Green.

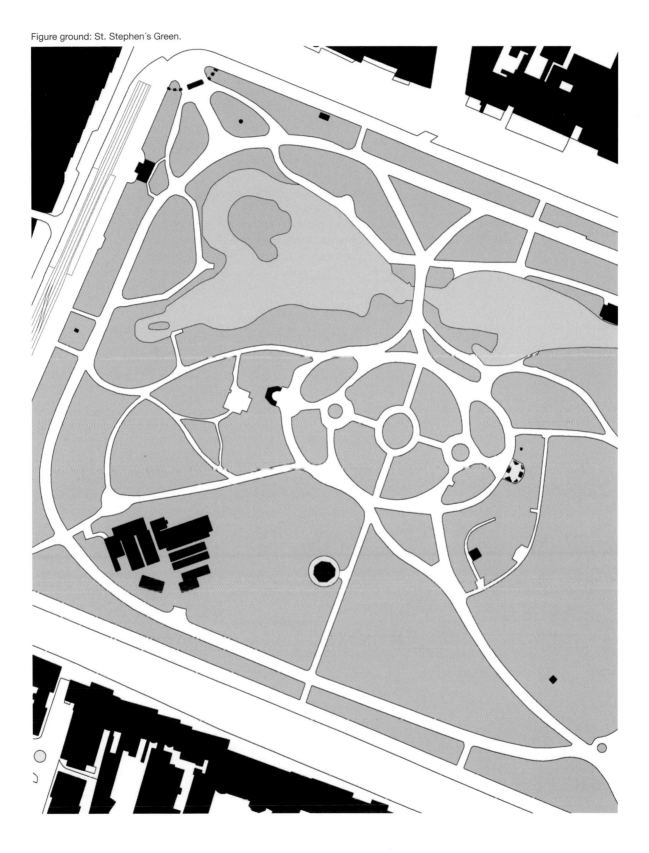

THIS GREEN

This green is a lung for a city,
This green is a place to walk and think,
And sit and listen to the poets being witty
Because poetry in Dublin flows like drink

And this green is a poem in an urban setting,
This green is a poem that scans and rhymes
Where you talk about remembering and forgetting
And you sit and sing about bygone times

Because every city needs a green like this
To pause for a moment in the city's throng
This green is a smile and this green is a kiss
And Dublin is the city where St. Stephen's Green belongs ...

Sketch, St. Stephen's Green.

a great many features which mark and celebrate the past of this place. These include the Fusiliers' Arch at the north-western corner, facing the top of Grafton Street, which commemorates the Royal Dublin Fusiliers who lost their lives in the Second Boer War; a bronze statue of Theobald Wolfe Tone, the father of Irish republicanism, who took part in the rebellion of 1798; another bronze statue of the Irish patriot Robert Emmet; a memorial to the Fenian leader Jeremiah O'Donovan Rossa; a Yeats garden; a bust of James Joyce; a memorial to the Great Famine; and, of course, a statue of Lord Ardilaun, the man who gave it to the people of Dublin. Fringing the gardens, notable historic buildings such as Iveagh House (headquarters of the Irish Department of Foreign Affairs), the Royal College of Surgeons, the Shelbourne Hotel, Loreto College, the Unitarian church and three gentlemen's clubs establish the social and civic credentials of the Green.

Today, in St. Stephen's Green the devil is in the details. As a place, it owes a great deal of its peaceful ambience to good traffic and event planning: recent changes in traffic management, including the introduction of the Luas tram system, have successfully limited vehicular traffic at least on one of its four sides, and parking and pavement finishes make for a high quality of environment around the perimeter of the green. Buildings that fringe the green itself date from several different periods, and the older ones have not been overly restored as is often the case with more perfectly preserved examples of Georgian squares. Contemporary adaptations of the layout of the park setting include a scented garden for the blind and partially sighted to enjoy, and every summer there is now an extensive programme of events including family days, music programmes, dancing, history and environment walks, magic, face-painting, and Punch and Judy shows.

The future of place

Place demands specificity and memorability. There has in the past two decades been a great deal of published writing about 'non-place' and the tendency of our modern cities to descend into vagueness and placelessness, particularly when they enter a post-industrial era. The rise of virtual locations and the increasingly mediated nature of our existence have also led to a greater attachment to the presentness and certainties of place. Of particular importance are places that provide comfort and belonging. However, when a place is too stage-managed it can serve to alienate rather than engender inhabitation and emotional commitment. Gaston Bachelard once argued that 'we do not change place, we change our nature',[4] and it would seem that in the first three examples chosen by The Academy of Urbanism we can see how the nature of our relationship to place is being successfully reworked and re-mapped.

Summer events in St. Stephen's Green.

References

1   Oldenburg, Ray, *The Great Good Place*, Marlowe & Co, 1999.
2   Raban, Jonathan, *Soft City*, Collins Harvill, 1974.
3   Hajer, Maarten and Reijndorp, Arnold, *In Search of the New Public Domain*, NAI Publishers, 2001.
4   Bachelard, Gaston, *The Poetics of Space*, Beacon Press, 1969.

Frank McDonald

Space! Place! Life!

What do we mean by public space? For most people, it would be a park or a square, a new civic plaza or a promenade. But as Jan Gehl likes to point out, the truth is that at least four-fifths of all public space in any city consists of its streets. And how we apportion their use speaks volumes about our urban sensibilities.[1]

Imagine a capital city where pedestrians rarely have to wait more than 30 seconds to cross a busy street, where bus and rail services run like clockwork, where there's no sign of serious traffic congestion and where 36 per cent of all commuters bike to work – on cycleways wide enough to travel two abreast. This urban utopia actually exists, and it's called Copenhagen. Roughly the same size as Dublin in terms of population, with 1.2 million people living in its metropolitan area, the city is a lot flatter, which facilitates cycling, but also two degrees latitude further north and on the Baltic Sea, which means it can be much colder in winter.

The big difference, of course, is that Copenhagen has been planned and managed with people in mind, whereas Dublin has not – at least, not since the 1920s. The walkable city of the late 18th century has expanded so wildly that most of its workforce has become totally car-dependent, especially those living at the extremities of a commuter belt stretching out 100 kilometres. Indeed, in November 2006, the European Environment Agency – coincidentally based in Copenhagen – cited Dublin's sprawl as a 'worst case scenario' of urban planning. It wanted to ensure that newer EU member states such as Poland would avoid making the Irish mistake of letting development run out of control, piggy-backing on new motorways built with funding from Brussels.

The Danish capital was the first to introduce the concept of a pedestrian street way back in 1962. Since then, Strøget – literally 'strolling street' – has become a template for many others all over the world. It has been extended over time into adjoining streets, while a seamless network of generously wide cycleways was created throughout the urban area, with an emphasis on the city centre. Jan Gehl, the veteran Copenhagen-based architect and urbanist, was the first to highlight the issue of pub-

Public life in Lyon: A busy thoroughfare in the early evening.

The pedestrian thoroughfare, Strøget, Copenhagen.

lic space in his influential book 'Life Between Buildings', and he still believes that cities need to be 're-conquered' to roll back the invasion of cars: 'If we want more sustainable cities, we need public realm, public transport and people living closer together.'

It's no coincidence that Copenhagen won the title 'European City of the Year' from the Royal Institute of British Architects in 2005 – primarily because it is a 'people-dominated city', as former RIBA president George Ferguson described it. The City Council even has a Department of Pedestrians, Public Spaces and Public Life, with its own action plan to pursue. The plan, adopted in 2005, aims to further improve conditions for pedestrians, making the city accessible to all, as well as create more spaces for playgrounds and leisure activities, such as the new promenade fringing the edge of an artificial island and lagoon on the Øresund, with 12 wind turbines offshore, or the imaginatively designed play spaces elsewhere in the city. Very few cyclists in Copenhagen wear helmets; they don't need to, because cycling is quite safe there. Similarly, pedestrians don't have to wait endlessly on footpaths; at most crossings they get the same amount of time as the traffic (30 seconds each). At College Street in the centre of Dublin, it's still 8 seconds for pedestrians and 96 seconds for traffic.

According to Oslo-based architect and academic Peter Butenschøn, public space has become 'the central battleground of our civilisation' and he wondered why it was not so hotly debated as 'opera houses, motorways and the secret life of celebrities'. Maybe, he speculated, 'it seems too polite'. Yet it's highly political: as Butenschøn observed, the first thing any dictatorship does is to ban the right to demonstrate. At an inspiring symposium in Copenhagen in September 2005, New York-based consultant Fred Kent said the movement to re-create public space as a 'dynamic human function, the essence of true democracy' was now a worldwide one. And he defined place-making as 'turning somewhere from a place you can't wait to get through to one you never want to leave'.

Take the transformation of 'dead and deserted' Melbourne into what its Director of Design and Culture, South African-born architect Rob Adams, describes as 'Australia's most interesting and vibrant city'. His mission, outlined in a 1985 strategic plan, is to turn Melbourne's central business district into a financially viable and environmentally sustainable 'central activities district'. And his motto – 'If we can design good streets, we will have good cities' – clearly works. Streets are alive with new shops, apartments and outdoor cafés, there are 75 festivals a year and the city has a major public art programme, including the Travellers memorial to Australia's waves of migration – giant stainless steel sculptures that move across a bridge. One of Adams' proudest boasts is that Melbourne has 'taken out 20 hectares of asphalt', in the form of roads and freeways that once scarred the city. A new levy on inner city commuter parking raised 19 million Australian dollars in 2006 and is expected to generate twice as much again in 2007 to fund transport initiatives, including more bus and cycle lanes.

Any city can have plans, but they're only good if they produce results. International branding of cities, with the use of 'signature' architecture, such as Bilbao

The Opera House, Copenhagen.

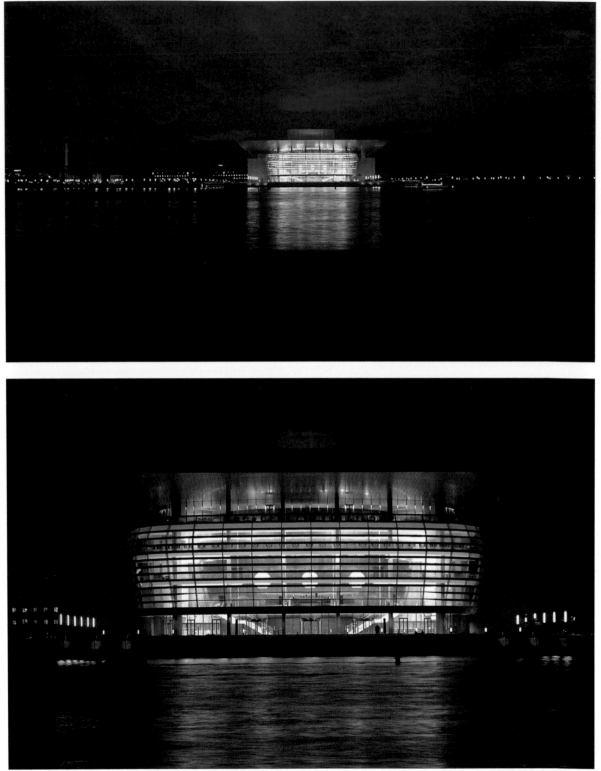

and its Guggenheim Museum, is almost essential in this competitive age, but the city must live up to its 'brand image', and renewal must also encompass the creation of quality public spaces.

Santiago Calatrava's Turning Torso tower (see page 18) has become an iconic trophy for Malmö, the southern Swedish city just half an hour by train from Copenhagen. A stunning piece of structural engineering, it rises to a height of 190 metres, twisting 90 degrees on the way up; it's the centrepiece of Malmö's Västra Hamnen (Western Harbour), which was once full of shipbuilding yards. The Torso may be a marker, but the real deal in Malmö is Klas Tham's urban plan – the one he kept faith with in spite of every obstacle thrown up by the market. Like so many redundant dockland areas, Västra Hamnen is being developed as a major extension of the city. It is now linked to Copenhagen by the Øresund bridge and tunnel, and is characterised by a remarkable architectural diversity, which derives from what its former chief planner Mats Olsson called a 'confetti city' approach – involving as many talented architects as possible.

The emphasis of the plan is on getting a good mix of uses. Five-storey apartment buildings, usually with shops or cafés at ground level, line the attractive waterfront promenade, which is now Malmö's favourite place for strolling; on sunny and warm Sunday afternoons, it is thronged with people of all ages, including young children. Amazingly, the entire area of Västra Hamnen is barrier-free. It is possible for visitors to walk anywhere, even into courtyards and small streets to the rear lined with terraced houses. There are no gates with swipe-card access; everywhere is public space. It also has a fine marina and skateboard park – a marvellous undulating landscape of shiny-smooth concrete, swooping with daredevil kids.

Even if its emblematic Torso had never been erected, the manner in which Västra Hamnen is being developed is the way to go. It will take many years to be built out, but any visitor can already see that it is heading in the right direction – a model of good urban design and sustainable development that really pays attention to the need for quality public space. As Jan Gehl observed in Copenhagen, the primary function of public space is as a meeting place, of people and of cultures. 'Some awful spaces are still being made because there are quite a few architects who never found out what it's all about. Others are being made with great care because we're getting better at it, but we really need to understand the issues.'

According to Stig Anderson, an Oslo-based landscape architect and digital art promoter, urban public spaces must offer 'texture, colour and sensuousness' – giving people different experiences as they move through the city, by day and by night. And in Copenhagen, a public life survey in 2005 revealed that a third of all activities in the city are happening at night.

Paris makes a show of light with its annual Nuit Blanche and the illumination of the Eiffel Tower, and Lyon has its Fête des Lumières – which translates as Festival of Light; à la Glasgow, it produced Radiance in the Merchant City,

Below and Right: Lyon by night.

featuring 'beautiful buildings illuminated by stunning light installations and cap-tivating visual artworks in unusual and unexpected places', as its brochure says.

Pasqual Maragall, the former Mayor of Barcelona, understood the need for public space and for spectacle. When he was first elected in 1982, he an-nounced that his vision was to 'turn Barcelona around to face the sea', and it was his inspirational drive to realise this vision – mainly by creating new public spaces – that won the Olympic Games for the city in 1992. It was Maragall who persuaded the Catalan diva, Monserrat Caballé, to team up with Fred-die Mercury for the great Barcelona concert at Montjuic in 1988, to celebrate the renewal of the city. He also sanctioned plans to rebuild Mies van der Rohe's German pavilion, originally built for the Barcelona Exposition in 1929 – reinstating an image imprinted on every architect's mind.

In Paris, meanwhile, François Mitterand was pursuing his *grands projets* – the Pyramid at the Louvre, the new Opera at Bastille and the Grand Arche that finally made a place of La Défense. These projects and others, including the Bibli-otheque nationale de France, also involved the

creation of new public spaces in a city that hardly needed further embellishment
but was wise enough to realise that it couldn't simply rest on its laurels. New public
parks were also key components of Mitterand's vision, best exemplified by the Parc
Citroën, with its fountains and selection of gardens, and the Parc de Bercy, fringed by
sensitively designed contemporary apartment buildings. These popular parks show
that the French landscaping tradition, so evident in the Place des Vosges, lives on in
different and exciting ways. The Pompidou Centre, which celebrated its 30th an-
niversary in January 2007, was the first truly sensational modern structure to be built
in Paris since the Eiffel Tower in 1889. But it was always more than a building; Renzo
Piano and Richard Rogers also created a sloping piazza, in homage to the Campo in
Siena, and it instantly became a hugely popular public space.

In Strasbourg they have some of the most beautiful trams in Europe. The inaugura-
tion of the city's tramway in 1994 did not merely mark the introduction of a new transport network but was used as a Trojan horse to lever major improvements in the urban environment, such as the pedestrians-only piazza on Place Kléber, which used to
carry 50,000 vehicles per day. A survey four years later found that nearly two-thirds of
the city's motorists believed that cars in towns are 'a thing of the past'. Strasbourg's
then mayor, Roland Ries, agreed: 'The city does not belong to the car. Cyclists and
pedestrians have more right to use the city.' If unlimited car use was to continue, he
warned, sprawl would turn our cities into 'formless heaps'. His predecessor, Catherine Trautmann, championed the most radical change in Strasbourg, with the avowed

Left: The Celestial Net, Royal Exchange Square, Glasgow.

Below: Parc du Bercy.

Above: Occasional spaces in the old town, Barcelona.

aim of 'reducing the hegemony of the car' by banning through-traffic from the city centre and improving public transport. After the tramway came into service, passenger numbers doubled within a few years and the bus network was replanned to link up with it.

All over Europe, cities are pursuing similar policies. 'They realise that unbridled use of cars for individual journeys is no longer compatible with easy mobility for the majority of citizens,' according to Ritt Bjerregaard, Mayor of Copenhagen and former EU Environment Commissioner. A switch to public transport also cuts air pollution and greenhouse gas emissions.

The small German city of Freiburg (population: 200,000) has shown how it is possible to virtually stop the rise in car use, even when car ownership is growing. Its success in 'taming the automobile' is due to restricting access by cars to the city centre, providing an integrated public transport system and strictly regulating development to keep the urban area compact.

Of course, land use and transport are inextricably linked – how we live and how we get around. And for us in Britain and Ireland, compact cities inevitably involve a cultural compromise between the traditional ideal of a two-storey house with front and back gardens, to which we still cling, and 'living on top of each other' in apartments, as our Continental cousins do.

Space must be created in inner city areas to make family living not only viable but also an attractive alternative to suburban norms. This can't be done simply by insisting on the provision of larger than average-sized apartments; a whole environment needs to be created at ground level to make it possible for couples with young children or teenagers to live in the city.

Ironically, one of the most progressive examples of how to cater for them comes from North America, rather than Europe. Bucking the trend that has seen so many North American cities turned into 'doughnuts' – hollowed-out centres surrounded by sprawling suburbs – Vancouver City Council adopted a set of guidelines on high-density housing for families with children in 1992 – long before we in Britain started thinking about it. The guidelines specify that such family housing should be located within 800 metres' walking distance of an elementary school, day-care centre and grocery shopping, and within 400 metres of a playground and public transport stop. Indeed, architects working in Vancouver were directed to 'design the whole environment with the safety needs of children in mind'.[2] For example, access to schools and amenities would involve providing a walking route free from barriers such as major unsignalled traffic junctions.

Left: Public life, Placa
Real, Barcelona.

Above: Tram passing
Place Kleiber, Stras-
bourg.

The guidelines also say that there should be a sufficient number of family
units in a project to give children peers to play with, to support the provision
of adequate amenities and encourage a sense of community. More than 20
hectares of new parks have been provided on the peninsula that encompasses
downtown Vancouver. These provide both active and passive recreation areas,
catering for ball games as well as strollers and people just sitting out. Some
20 kilometres of the waterfront has been laid out for promenades and cycle
tracks, in furtherance of the city's 'Living First' policy.

At least 45,000 people have moved downtown since 1990 – more than dou-
bling its population – and most of the new residents are living in 'condo towers'
that rise to 30 storeys or more. Tall and slender, with a maximum floorplate of
650 square metres and no more than six or eight apartments per floor, these
towers are all about access to daylight and views. They are usually set on podi-
ums, with shops and restaurants at ground-floor level, flanked by three-storey
'row houses' – terraced houses, as we would call them – to cater for people
who prefer their own door onto the street. And from the beginning, adequate

provision was made for social and affordable housing, which accounts for 17 per cent of the total.

The skyline is also being composed, like a piece of music. In the 1970s, there was a basic rule that the tallest buildings should be in the centre. This was refined in the 1980s to protect 20 key 'view corridors', to retain its relationship with the water that surrounds the city as well as the mountains to the north, where the Winter Olympics were held in 2010. No wonder Vancouver was voted 'Best City in the Americas' in 2004 by readers of *Condé Nast Traveller*. And because of its emphasis on promoting active recreation, it also won an award from the Canadian Heart and Stroke Foundation for being statistically healthier than other cities, with only a 10 per cent rate of obesity compared to the national average of 30 per cent. 'Our view is that the municipality should set out the vision and collaborate with everyone to achieve it,' said Larry Beasley, the city's director of planning. Major development proposals are reviewed by an urban design panel, and almost all projects are designed by local architects; the city didn't feel any compelling need to sign up 'starchitects' like Calatrava, Gehry or Libeskind.

The Bechels in Freibourg.

Hockey teams playing against the high-rise backdrop of downtown Vancouver.

Such self-sufficiency, matched by a high level of community involvement, is also very evident in the three towns reviewed by David Rudlin – from the numerous local trusts in Ludlow to the regeneration partnerships in Lincoln and the community spirit in St. Ives. It is also a characteristic of the neighbourhoods of Clifton in Bristol and the Merchant City in Glasgow considered by Brian Evans. What's crucial, however, is to engage the public in working towards sustainable development at a city scale. Few of the statutory mechanisms we have, in Britain or Ireland, are adequate to this task, so we must seek new models of public participation to enable ordinary citizens to get involved. And one of the most successful of these models is in San Francisco.

SPUR, an acronym for the San Francisco Planning and Urban Research Association, has been in operation in one form or another since 1957. Over the past 50 years, it has mediated in conflicts over plans for San Francisco, promoted a consensus approach and helped to build a strong sense of *civitas* in a city that is arguably even more fractious than Dublin, Edinburgh or London. One of SPUR's initiatives is the Citizen Planning Institute, a public policy conference series covering such issues as transportation, downtown development and 'ecological urbanism'. It brings in leading thinkers from around the USA – or around the world – to provide decision-makers with a broad perspective on how other cities are coping with challenges.

Hands-on planning community engagement.

With nine neighbourhood plans under way and more in the pipeline, San Francisco has made a major commitment to local area-based planning. SPUR's Urban Planning Committee coordinates its involvement in all of these neighbourhood planning efforts, as well as its work on citywide planning, with a special focus on the city's 'general plan' for development. This plan deals with housing, commerce and industry, recreation and open space, community facilities, transportation, public safety, environmental protection, urban design and the arts. Its overarching objectives are to protect the special character and quality of San Francisco, including its architectural heritage, as well as the city's neighbourhood life.

SPUR also has a Sustainable Development Committee (chaired by landscape architect Katherine Howard) which aims to influence public policy. Its membership includes people from a wide variety of backgrounds such as architects, ecologists, urban planners, water-use specialists, engineers and even city officials, but it's open to everyone to join. With the twin aims of preventing suburban sprawl and promoting San Francisco as a great urban centre, SPUR is campaigning to speed up the 'Muni' (municipal transport system) by at least 25 per cent on core routes, to make it 'rock-solid reliable'. This would involve 'getting cars out of the way' of buses and giving public transport priority at all intersections. Above all, however, what the SPUR model offers is the prospect of building a civic consensus to set long-term goals and 'move forward sustainably', according to Dubliner David O'Gorman, who lived in San Francisco for eight years.

However, the public needs help in visualising how things might be; plans, sections, elevations and perhaps a model or computer-generated perspectives are not enough. In Glasgow, a digital, three-dimensional model of the city's core – developed by Doug Pritchard, Head of Visualisation at Glasgow School of Art – could bridge the comprehension gap. Buildings were laser scanned and then slotted into what may be the most detailed model of its kind in the world; one of its great benefits is that new schemes can be judged in their context. Not only would digital packages like this facilitate meaningful public participation in planning; they could also be made available to schools so that the younger generation can develop their visual awareness and gain a deeper understanding of space, place and life in the city.

References

1   Gehl, Jan, *Life Between Buildings*, 1971 (republished 1987, 1996).

2   *High Density Housing for Families with Children Guidelines*, City of Vancouver Planning Department, (1992).

About The Academy
of Urbanism

Background
The Academy Manifesto

The Academy of Urbanism brings together a group of thinkers and practitioners involved in the social, cultural, economic, political and physical development of our villages, towns and cities, across Great Britain and Ireland. The Academy was formed in February 2006 to extend urban discourse beyond built environment professionals and to create an autonomous, politically independent and self-funded learned voice. We aim to advance the understanding and practice of urbanism by promoting a culture of scholarship through evidence-based inquiry, providing an inclusive forum for dialogue across all disciplines, sharing knowledge with the community and our peers and nurturing, recognising and rewarding excellence in achievement.

Principles

01 Successful urbanism is the result of a collective vision, realised through creative and enduring relationships between the community, government, developers and professionals involved in its design, delivery, governance and maintenance.

02 The culture, or cultures of the people and the ecology of the place must be expressed at a human scale and through both physical and social structures.

03 The identity, diversity and full potential of the community must be supported spiritually, physically and visually to sustain a sense of collective ownership, belonging and civic pride.

04 Vibrant streets and spaces, defined by their surrounding buildings and with their own distinct character, should form a coherent interconnected network of places that support social interaction and display a hierarchy of private, commercial and civil functions.

05 There must be a permeable street network with pedestrian priority that gives maximum freedom of movement and a good choice of means of transport.

06 Essential activities must be within walking distance and there should be a concentration of activity around meeting places.

07 Places must provide a diversity of functions, tenure, facilities and services; have a mix of building designs and types; and include a variety of appropriately scaled districts and neighbourhoods.

08 The social, cultural and economic needs of all inhabitants must be capable of being met without detriment to the quality of the lives of others.

09 Security should be achieved by organising the urban environment in ways that encourage people to act in a civil and responsible manner.

10 The pedestrian environment should be closely associated with active frontages at street level and there should be an appropriate intensity of use in all areas at all times.

11 The design of spaces and buildings should be influenced by their context and seek to enhance local character and heritage while simultaneously responding to current-day needs, changes in society and cultural diversity.

12 The public realm and civil institutions must be supported and protected by sound and inclusive processes that respond to the local community and changing economic and social conditions.

13 Decision-making for the ongoing development and management of the urban fabric must engage stakeholders and the local community through public participation and dissemination

14 Diverse, accessible, affordable and active villages, towns and cities will encourage successful commercial activity, promote prosperity and support the well-being of their inhabitants.

15 New and existing places must respect, enhance and respond to their local topography, geology and climate and connect to the natural environment within and around them.

16 Urban parks and other landscaped areas should provide space for recreation, encourage biodiversity and help support a balanced environment.

17 New urban forms should be capable of adaptation over time to meet changing needs and to promote the continued use of existing resources, including the built environment.

18 The built environment must seek to minimise the use of carbon-based products, energy and non-renewable resources.

THE ACADEMY OF URBANISM

Where did it come from?

The Academy was launched in February 2006 and is a high-level, cross-sector group of individuals and organisations that champions, through discourse, research, education and awards, the cause of good-quality urbanism, throughout Great Britain and Ireland.

The Academy seeks to promote and disseminate lessons about good urbanism and to work in partnership with other agencies and organisations that can assist in delivering best practice on the ground.

The concept grew from a core group of multi-disciplinary participants, brought together originally through the RIBA's Urbanism and Planning Group, with the intention of creating an Academy, originally of one hundred people, to be renewed and updated over time.

What does it do?

Through its Academicians, the Academy promotes scholarship through evidence-based inquiry, fosters an inclusive environment for cross-disciplinary discourse, provides educational events focused on good urbanism, and validates good places and practice through The Urbanism Awards.

Who is involved?

The Academicians are drawn from a diverse range of professional, developer, academic and community backgrounds. Academicians are both enthusiasts and credible practitioners in their relevant fields, able to both help judge and disseminate lessons in good-quality urbanism. The culture of the organisation emanates from its Academicians, who are united in a committed obligation to share and disseminate their knowledge for the benefit of communities, villages, town and cities.

How does it work?

Individuals become Academicians by invitation and pay an annual fee to belong to the Academy. In support of the Academy's Education Programme Academicians agree to initiate, or participate in, at least one 'badged' activity or event per year, promoting the practice and understanding of good urbanism. The Academy also publishes its own annual anthology, *Learning from Place*, drawing on its Awards programme as source material.

How does it fit with other bodies?

The Academy aims to fill a distinct role and not duplicate or contradict the primary roles of other bodies and organisations. It has links to other bodies, professions and the philosophical aspirations of others, and is supported by named representatives from a number of affiliated organisations. These currently include CABE, The HCA, Architecture and Design Scotland, the Design Commission for Wales, RIBA, RIAI, the Housing Corporation, South East England Development Agency (SEEDA), Yorkshire Forward, the Urban Design Group and the Urban Forum, Ireland.

The Academy is therefore not a completely stand-alone entity. It is a member-based network and is therefore different from the professions (RIBA, RIAI, RIAS, RTPI, RICS, etc.) who may share some of the same objectives, but who have a wider remit and are based upon technical entry levels and professional competencies.

The Academy is also different from CABE, as well as Architecture and Design Scotland and the Design Commission for Wales, in that it is not a government-created and funded body, but an independent network of key individuals and representatives.

Because of its cross-sectoral high-level voluntary network, the Academy is able to cut across professional and other boundaries, making connections between research, policy and the rhetorical aspects of advocacy and design, development, investment and implementation.

The Urbanism Awards

Through The Urbanism Awards, the Academy is creating a body of evidence-based research in Cities, Towns, Neighbourhoods, Streets and Places, that will be used, together with other exemplars, to further teaching, research and dissemination of best practice in urbanism.

Each year, the Academy shortlists three candidates in each category that are then visited, and studied thoroughly using the following criteria:

- Governance
- Local Character and Distinctiveness
- User Friendliness
- Commercial Success and Viability
- Environmental and Social Sustainability
- Functionality

Board and Academicians

Directors
John Thompson (Chairman), Pam Alexander, Chris Brett, Prof. Brian Evans, George Ferguson CBE, Dick Gleeson, Prof. Kevin Murray, Trevor Osborne, John Worthington.

Academicians
Robert Adam, Marcus Adams, Lynda Addison OBE, Linda Aitken, John Aitkin, Prof. Chris Alexander, Sandy Allcock, Ben Allgood, Ian Angus, Debbie Aplin, Jasvir Atwal, Jeff Austin, Chris Balch, David Balcombe, Sue Ball, Jonathan Barker, Yolande Barnes, Alistair Barr, Prof. Lawrence Barth, Jemma Basham, Trevor Beattie, Ian Beaumont, Matthew Bedward, Steven Bee, Andrew Beharrall, John Bell, Michael Bennett, Duncan Berntsen, John Betty, Joost Beunderman, Richard Bickers, David Bishop, David FL Bishop, Noemi Blager, Sergey Bobkov, Alan Boldon, Ben Bolgar, Duncan Bowie, Guy Briggs, Ross Brodie, Jonathan Brown, Patricia Brown, Mark Burgess, Andrew Burrell, Jonathan Burroughs, Prof. Georgia Butina Watson, Stephen Byfield, Rod Cahill, Robert Camlin, Kelvin Campbell, Fiona Campbell, Steve Canadine, Tony Carey, Emma Cariaga, James Carr, Sam Cassels, Manish Chande, Sarah Chaplin, Prof. James Chapman, Richard Charge, Prof. David Chiddick, Nick Childs, Harry Christophides, Prof. Greg Clark, Tom Clarke, Adrian Cole, Marc Cole, Robert Coles, Garry Colligan, Paul Collins, Martin Colreavy, Peter Connolly, Karen Cooksley, Nick Corbett, Rob Cowan, David Cowans, Linda Curr, Ned Cussen, Jennie Daly, Debbie Dance, Phil Darcy, Prof. Trevor Davies, Rob Davies, Philip Davies, Michael Davis, Paul Davis, Simon Davis, Mark Davy, Eric Dawson, Guy Denton, Neil DePrez, Ben Derbyshire, Andrew Dick, Hank Dittmar, Sir Jeremy Dixon, Andrew Dixon, Nick Dodd, Mike Donnelly, Martin Downie, Roger Dowty, Peter Drummond, Duncan Ecob, Luke Engleback, Karen Escott, Prof. Graeme Evans, Nick Ewbank, Dr. Nicholas Falk, Sir Terry Farrell, Jaimie Ferguson, Darryl Flay, John Foddy, Sue Foster, Bernie Foulkes, Simon Foxell, Alan Francis, Jerome Frost, William Fulford, Jeremy Gardiner, John Geeson, Lia Ghilardi, Andy Gibbins, Prof. Mike Gibson, Bruce Gilbreth, Ian Gilzean, Herbert Girardet, Christopher Glaister, Francis Glare, Stephen Gleave, Keith Gowenlock, Gerry Grams, Colin Grant, Gary Grant, Mark Greaves, Stephen Greenberg, Ali Grehan, Simon Guest, Silvia Gullino, Prof. Stuart Gulliver, Patrick Gulliver, Paul Guzzardo, Trutz Haase, Susan Hallsworth, Pete Halsall, Tim Hancock, Malcolm Hankey, Annette Hards, Dr. Matthew Hardy, Dr. Catherine Harper, Geoff Haslam, Helen Hayes, Prof. Richard Hayward, Nicholas Hayward, Peter Heath, Prof. Michael Hebbert, David Height, Wayne Hemingway, Peter Hibbert, Stephen Hill, Jason Hill, Marie Hodgson, Tim Holden, Eric Holding, Sam Howes, Stephen Howlett, Jun Huang, David Hughes, John Hyland, Delton Jackson, Philip Jackson, Sarah Jarvis, Sir Simon Jenkins, Philip Jones, Stephen Jordan, Simon Kaplinsky, Prashant Kapoor, Dr. Kayvan Karimi, Andy Karski, Jonathan Kendall, David Kennedy, Angus Kennedy, John Kennedy, Sir Bob Kerslake, Ros Kerslake, Hugo Kirby, Gary Kirk, Jim Kirkwood, Liezel Kruger, Chris Lamb, Cllr Andrew Lamont, Charles Landry, Derek Latham, Diarmaid Lawlor, Adrian Lee, Sir Richard Leese, Mick Leggett, John Letherland, David Levitt, Michael Lewis, Harry Lewis, Martin Lippitt, Michael Liverman, David Lock, John Lord, Vivien Lovell,

Fergus Low, Michael Lowndes, Joanna Lucas, David Lumb, Barra Mac Ruairi, Tom Macartney, Pol MacDonald, Robin Machell, Roger Madelin, Riccardo Marini, Andreas Markides, Alona Martinez-Perez, Mark Massey, James McAdam, Richard McCarthy, Frank McDonald, Kevin McGeough, Marie-Thérèse McGivern, Nigel McGurk, Craig McLaren, Alan Mee, Alastair Mellon, Ian Mellor, David Miles, Stephan Miles-Brown, Willie Miller, Neil Monaghan, Prof. Ruth Morrow, Elizabeth Motley, Ronnie Muir, John Muir, Eugene Mullan, John Mullin, Andy Munro, Claudia Murray, Hugh Murray, Peter Murray, Chris Murray, Vivek Nanda, Peter Nears, Marko Neskovic, Lora Nicolaou, John Nordon, William Nowlan, Helen O'Doherty, Simon Ogden, Killian O'Higgins, Sean O'Laoire, Chris Oldershaw, Tiago Oliveira, John O'Regan, Clara Overes, Susan Parham, Chris Parkin, Prof. Richard Parnaby, Richard Pearce, Adam Peavoy, Prof. Alan Penn, Alison Peters, Hugh Petter, Jon Phipps, James Pike, Ben Plowden, Demetri Porphyrios, Jonathon Porritt, Dr. Sergio Porta, Prof. David Porter, David Powell, Robert Powell, Sunand Prasad, John Prevc, David Prichard, Paul Prichard, Rhona Pringle, Douglas Pritchard, Mark Raisbeck, Peter Ralph, Clive Rand, Mike Rawlinson, Tony Reddy, Richard Rees, Richard Reid, Ingrid Reynolds, Christopher Rhodes, Anthony Rifkin, Prof. Marion Roberts, Prof. Peter Roberts OBE, Stuart Robinson, Dickon Robinson, Bryan Roe, Lord Richard Rogers, Angela Rolfe, Pedro Roos, Anna Rose, Graham Ross, Sarah Royle-Johnson, David Rudlin, Robert Rummey, Gerard Ryan, Prof. Andrew Ryder, Robert Sakula, Rhodri Samuel, Ivor Samuels, Andrew Sanderson, Hilary Satchwell, Jamie Saunders, Biljana Savic, David Schwarz, Dominic Scott, Toby Shannon, Barry Shaw, Richard Shaw, Keith Shearer, Anthony Shoults, Ron Sidell, Paul Simkins, Dr. Richard Simmons, David Slater, Dr. Lindsay Smales, Jonathan Smales, Jim Sneddon, Alastair Snow, Adrian Spawforth, Jerry Spencer, Andy Spracklen, Chris Standish, Alan Stewart, Martin Stockley, Andrew Stokes, Tim Stonor, Peter Studdert, Janet Sutherland, Mick Sweeney, Nicholas Sweet, Stephen Talboys, David Tannahill, Ian Tant, Prof. Robert Tavernor, Nick Taylor, David Taylor, Mike Taylor, David Taylor, Sandy Taylor, Ed Taylor, Catherine Teeling, Robert Thompson, Kirsteen Thomson, John Thorp, Jeremy Till, Rob Tincknell, Andrew Tindsley, Andrea Titterington, Ian Tod, Tricia Topping, Stephen Tucker, Iain Tuckett, Dr. Richard Turkington, Jonathan Turner, Chris Twomey, Peter Udall, Julia Unwin, Valli van Zijl, Atam Verdi, Andy von Bradsky, John Wakefield, Ian Wall, Russell Wallis, Ann Wallis, David Warburton, Prof. Martyn Ware, Paul Warner, Nick Wates, Rosemary Westbrook, Duncan Whatmore, Craig White, Lindsey Whitelaw, Patricia Willoughby, Marcus Wilshere, James Wilson, Simon Wilson, Chris Winter, Godfrey Winterson, Matt Wisbey, David Woods, Nick Woolley, Linda Wride, Nick Wright, Ian Wroot, Tony Wyatt, Wei Yang, Bob Young, Roger Zogolovitch.

Sponsors
Allanvale Land, Architecture + Design Scotland, Barton Willmore, Dublin City Council, Evans Property Group, Glasgow Housing Association, Highland, Howard de Walden Estate, Kevin Murray Associates, Land Securities, The Muir Group, Peel Holdings, Ptarmigan Land, Savills, Taylor Young, The Trevor Osborne Property Group, WYG Planning and Design.

Supporters-in-Kind
Alan Baxter & Associates, Barton Willmore, BDP, Charles Russell Solicitors, Church House Conference Centre, Ecobuild, John Thompson & Partners, PPS Group, Prentis & Co, RUDI, Space Syntax, Terry Farrell & Partners, Tibbalds Planning and Urban Design, URBED.

Picture Credits

Cover Photo: Brick Lane (Detail) -
John Thompson

All photographs except for those listed below taken by **John Thompson** during The Academy of Urbanism assessment visits.

All drawings created by **David (Harry) Harrison** and plans created by **Joe Wood**.

All images copyright of **The Academy of Urbanism** except for:

Introduction:
Wither an Academy of Urbanism?
p.11-12 photos Brian Evans

Space? Place? Life?
p.13,14,16,21: Photos Brian Evans
p.15,17: Photos Central Scotland Forest Trust

Cities: Continuity & Change
p.25,29,33,35,40,41: Photos Brian Evans

Towns: Learning from Ludlow, Lincoln & St. Ives
p.43-46, 54,51,55,60: photos David Rudlin
p.49 Aerial photo © Google
p.53 Aerial photo © Lincoln City Council
p.56,59: photos Richard Shaw

Neighbourhoods: The basic building block of the City
p. 62 Image courtesy of Glasgow City Council
p.64, 74: photos Brian Evans
p.68 image courtesy of Glasgow City Council
p.69 Image courtesy of Gillespies

Great Streets
p.81,83,86,93,94: photo David Taylor
p81: Aerial photos © Google
p83: photos Brian Evans

Places
p.105,108,114: Aerial photos © Google
p.117 photo Paul Keogh

Space! Place! Life
p.119,120,122, 124,125,128, 130: Photos Brian Evans
p.126,132: Images courtesy   of Gillespies
p.127: Photo Paul Keogh
p.129,231: Photo Frank McDonald
132: Photos Yorkshire Forward

Ludlow

Glasgow

Borough Market